So we do not lose heart. Though our outer self is wasting away, our inner self is being renewed day by day. For this light momentary affliction is preparing for us an eternal weight of glory beyond all comparison, as we look not to the things that are seen but to the things that are unseen. For the things that are seen are transient, but the things that are unseen are eternal (2 Corinthians 4:16-18).

Ron —

May these words add
Salt to your journey of
faith!

Gordon

LIVING
BEYOND THE
PAIN

LIVING BEYOND THE PAIN

ISBN 978-0-9855268-0-1
eISBN 978-0-9855268-1-8

Published by SELLEY ENTERPRISES, LLC

Cover and interior design by Nick Lee
Cover photo by bryancolephoto.com
Back cover author photo © Cassidy Brooke

Printed in the United States of America
First Edition 2012

1 2 3 4 5 6 7 8 9 10

050412

GORDON SELLEY

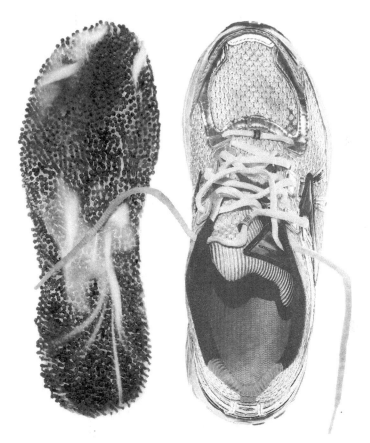

LIVING
BEYOND THE
PAIN

INSIGHTS FOR YOUR JOURNEY
OF TRANSFORMATION

Contents

Author's Preface

I wish I had the power to snap my fingers and instantly erase all your hurts and disappointments. But unfortunately, I can't alleviate your physical, emotional or spiritual pains.

What I can do is to share my own story—my own "Journey of Transformation"—with you. I think you will discover that my experience of having to confront seemingly unmanageable pain and insurmountable challenges isn't that much different from yours, especially if you feel stuck in some area of your life.

I have written this book for you so that it might serve as a guide to a better life. I believe the insights in these pages may help you change your life, because that's the point. Transformational change is possible for you, no matter what!

May this book encourage and help you on your own "Journey of Transformation!"

From Deserts of Despair to Rivers of Life

More than a quarter million books were published in the United States last year. Do we really need another?

I have no burning desire to write. I have plenty to keep me busy. So why subject myself to such an arduous process? Because I believe this little book you now hold in your hands can help you address and possibly overcome some of the most formidable challenges in your life.

That's because this book conveys lessons I learned after experiencing a traumatic series of catastrophes in my life. I went from feeling I was on top of the world to experiencing breakdowns in my health, my work, my finances and my relationships. I went from enjoying a good life to being lower than low, wracked by both severe physical pain and the kind of emotional sorrow that makes you feel like crawling into a hole and staying there forever.

Have you ever been to the Sahara Desert? I don't know why you would visit this furnace that covers three million square miles of Africa. But we have all seen movies (*Lawrence of Arabia*) or TV shows ("Man vs. Wild") that portray people battling blinding light, oppressive heat and throat-shredding dryness.

People who find themselves in a desert will do anything for a drink of cool, clear water. Often they can be fooled into thinking a big pool of water lies far off in the distance. Scientists call this a mirage, which is an optical phenomenon that bends light rays and plays with our perceptions. Like many people, I have pursued plenty of mirages during my life.

The insights I would like to share with you in this book are not mirages. Some of them may fit you better than others, but each and every one of them has greatly impacted my life, and I believe they can do the same for you, no matter what kinds of pain and suffering and tragedy you may have experienced or are experiencing now.

Come along and see for yourself.

When Life Doesn't Work

Here's my true story. In the 1990s I felt like life was about as good as it could be. I was a successful chiropractic doctor with a wonderful practice of loyal clients and a very professional staff. I was disciplined and hard working, so it wasn't unusual for me to work 12-14 hours a day, sometimes getting to the office as early as 3:00 a.m. to get a head start on the day's work. The pace was grueling, but I greeted each new day with optimism, anxious to go out and make my mark on the world.

After work, I played hard. Golf was my passion, and I was trying to develop my game. Whenever possible, I would try and squeeze in 18 holes at the country club, after exchanging my tailor-made suit for snazzy golf clothes.

I would work on weekends, too, all the while trying to make room for some family time on our boat or traveling throughout our beautiful state of Colorado.

But there wasn't much down time. I spent many weekends taking post-graduate courses to help me acquire the board certifications needed to take my practice to the next level. I felt I could be the best at anything I wanted to do, and what I wanted was to be the best chiropractor and businessman I could possibly be. I considered myself cutting-edge, and kept up with all the developments in my field by reading academic journals, attending seminars and trying new methods.

I had strong ambition and was driven to be the best so I could rise above the socioeconomic realities of my parents. My dad was an admired schoolteacher, having taught both high school and college, and my mother worked various administrative assistant jobs. Both parents loved me, but I felt their lives were uncomfortably hard, especially trying to raise five kids. I wanted to enjoy a better standard of living than the one I grew up with, and I was doing so.

So far, so good. I felt I could outwork anybody as I took my career to the next level, and the next, and the next. Plus, I felt that God was on my side. I guess you could say I was a religious person. I felt my faith contributed to my overall success, and that my success was a proof of my faith.

Everything flipped upside down. First, I watched my marriage fall apart. Then, over the course of two months, I suffered two traumatic neck injuries that left me in horrendous pain and unable to work. Before long, it was as if all hell broke loose. Things I once took for granted became overwhelming obstacles to me. Even the daily stroll to the mailbox caused me great panic. That's because my mailbox was overflowing with staggering bills I couldn't pay and a never-ending stream of insurance forms I needed to fill out detailing my injuries.

Just when it seemed things couldn't get any worse, they did. The I.R.S. came knocking on my door after I had closed down my business. All the money and property and clothes and toys I had worked so hard and so long to acquire seemed to disappear overnight.

One thing I did have was plenty of medical procedures and doctor bills. I underwent multiple neck surgeries involving the removal of several of my disks and some of my bone, the insertion of a titanium plate, and the introduction of a wire mesh "cage" to hold everything together. Concurrently,

I was undergoing several pain-mediating blocks and taking so many pain medications that I became fat, sluggish, and depressed.

Perhaps more surprisingly, my suffering revealed to me the shallowness of many of my relationships. I lost connection with most of my friends, associates and even people at church. When your life has been turned upside down by failure and pain, people don't want to be near you. They're afraid your bad luck will rub off on them. I felt like a leper that no one wanted to touch or be near. People said they would pray for me, but they mainly wanted to keep their distance.

This made it easier for me to point the finger at God and blame him for my misfortunes. But the more I ranted and raved and blamed anyone but myself, the more I could sense that I was hardening my heart to the possibility of recovery.

As I sat on the floor in a one-bedroom apartment with my few possessions—mattress, lamp, TV, Bible and a few of my son's toys—I considered the bad soap opera my life had become. If there was a form of pain, I was experiencing it: physical, mental, emotional, financial and spiritual.

I didn't think there was any way I could ever get close to where I was before. That's when I began to seriously contemplate suicide.

The story could have ended there. I'm glad it didn't.

A Drop of Water in the Desert

At this stage in my life, I felt that transformation seemed far out of reach. And, the truth of the matter is, it was.

But, if there's one good thing you can say about pain and suffering, it's that they help you focus. People talk about the refiner's fire. I felt like I was being tortured by the searing flames from a giant blowtorch.

While my body and everything in the external world was being destroyed, my spirit was being awakened. In the midst of my trials I was being humbled, and it was about time. Gordon was finally beginning to see that the world was not all about him and his success, even though I had long been convinced it was. This newfound humility caused me to look beyond myself for a change.

It was at that point in my desert of despair and pain that I experienced hope, and it wasn't a mirage. I needed hope more than anything else right then, because I had given up on trying to improve my circumstances. I felt I had totally exhausted all my options for something better.

For me, hope finally came when I realized that it wasn't too late for me to change. Yes, I had fallen. Yes, I had lost everything I had worked to build up. Yes, I was on my own.

But was I really alone? Somehow, long after I had spent all the resources I had, I received help from an unexpected source. Simply put, I knew that God had extended his hand to me. After exhausting all of my puny resources, I was being given an opportunity to tap into something much bigger and much more powerful than little old me.

This unexpected infusion of hope was like being in a desert and tasting a drop of clear, cool water. That one drop didn't quench my thirst, but it gave me hope because I figured where there was one drop of water there must be another.

That was all I needed at the time: the *hope* that something better was possible.

As slim as the evidence was for this potential transformation, I believed it, and I trusted it. And if I can convey anything to you at the beginning of this book, it is that you, too, can experience your drop of water in the desert. You can experience refreshing hope in the face of sorrow. You can change your life even though the prospects for transformation don't seem great.

Let me explain.

It Isn't Too Late For You

Can I ask you a few questions?

Are you too injured to believe in healing?

Are you weighed down by debt or other financial worries?

Are you too overweight and discouraged to work at losing those extra pounds?

Have you botched all your chances for a fresh start in life?

Whenever I attempted to step out toward healing, I usually fell flat on my face. I felt like the Apostle Peter when he got out of the boat and tried to walk on the water. After a few successful steps, Peter looked down at the water. As his doubts rose up, he was soon submerged under the weight of disbelief.

Similarly, when I tried to incorporate more physical exercise into my life, I usually paid for it with more pain, lack of sleep and the need for additional bed rest. The same can be said for dieting and how I failed at losing weight, time and time again.

As far as re-entering the work force being disabled, it felt like I kept drowning in a sea of despair, as my physical limitations hindered me from practically every occupational possibility.

At church one Sunday, the pastor talked about something the Bible called the "abundant life." I didn't know exactly what that was, but it sounded better than what I had. Are you *willing* to live a life that is more abundant than the one you are living today? If so, you have at least a drop of hope, and any drop is precious in a desert of despair.

Making the Change

Make no mistake about it: the "Journey of Transformation" is not for the faint of heart, no matter how much divine assistance you believe you'll receive.

It takes incredible courage to see life from a different perspective and then to actually take that initial step toward a newly formed reality. To progress forward with the second step is even more daring, and so on down the path into a new journey.

Moving from old habits to establishing new patterns of living does not happen by mere coincidence. Neither is this process of change something that can be designed like an architectural blueprint or purchased through a self-help seminar.

If there's one thing I can do through the pages of this book, it is to meet you in that place where all faith in the future is gone.

I want to reach you in that place where things seem hopeless.

I want to shine a light into that place where you hide when you're broken and have experienced a real crisis of faith.

But most of all, I wish to share with you a few treasures I've discovered about the mysteries behind the transformed life.

Transformation is possible when we allow ourselves to be tapped by the wondrous power of God. Transformation is possible when our heart-wrenching confessions break the chains from our inconsolable parts. Transformation is possible when our old, tattered nature is miraculously converted into a new and improved life.

The purpose of this book is to challenge you and help you press beyond your resistance; to overcome your own version of pain and darkness; and to make the necessary adjustments to regain victory in life again.

Take it from me: it is never too late to change who you are and what you're doing. Even though I had fallen to a place of hopelessness, it wasn't too late for me. Miraculous change can and does happen! No matter where you are in your life.

Let's Get Started!

Isn't it time to get on the path of healthy living?

My experience is a testament that it is possible to drink from the oasis in the desert. Each step forward doesn't have to be met with two steps backward.

Are you willing to give life another try? Are you willing to re-capture the possibilities of living a meaningful life? If so, your time is now. Let's begin the "Journey of Transformation" together!

PART ONE

One

•

How Did I Get Here?

I vividly remember the day my neurosurgeon labeled me as *"totally and permanently disabled."*

It was very surreal. Although I had grown accustomed to wrestling with debilitating pain, I had never envisioned myself as being "disabled"; nor did I fully digest how this glum prognosis might impact my life.

As my doctor tried to explain the technical details about total and permanent disability, my brain literally shut down like a computer on overload. I felt completely empty, defeated and resigned to nothingness. Instead of hearing what my doctor had to say, all I could hear was my pounding heartbeat, which picked up speed the longer I listened to his explanation about the world I was about to enter—a world filled with pain, deprivation and loneliness.

The irony is this.

Previously, I had been the doctor, clinically explaining what permanent disability would mean to some of my own patients. I was well acquainted with the many details of the disability assessments that were required to determine permanent impairment ratings. I was very familiar with the uncomfortable feelings that arise when a doctor must inform patients that they will likely endure painful suffering that will effectively prevent them from living out productive and active lives. Uncomfortably, the tables were turned. Instead of being the one who delivered the bad news, I had now become the recipient.

Up until that moment, my life had been a series of efforts to push myself to higher and higher levels of achievement and success. Hitting rock bottom was a new experience for me. Everybody wants to talk to winners. We want to know the keys to their success. But nobody wants to hear from the downtrodden. No one seems to care what they think or feel. No one asks if they have anything worthwhile to share.

I certainly experienced this myself. Once I was officially labeled as disabled, I became aware of disability's discriminating power. No one ever asked me what it was like to become fat and fragile as I tried to cope with incapacitating pain. Nobody wondered what it was like for me to be downgraded from doctor to patient. Not one person sought out my insights on the transition from being passionately productive to seeking whatever contentment I could in a drastically scaled-down version of life.

It is understandable our insensitivity toward those who are down and out often springs from the superficiality of our own lives. When we focus on the outward appearances of life rather than the deeper realities of the heart, we rarely consider that becoming *fully* human might require hitting rock bottom first. When I was required to get up-close and personal with the bedrock of life, this brought me to a much deeper place than I had experienced while automatically climbing to the pinnacle of success.

But I didn't reach this conclusion while sitting in the doctor's office receiving his verdict. It would take time. Meanwhile, there was no way around my predicament. I was disabled, and now I had better start figuring out how to make the transition from the life I had once enjoyed to the uncertain life that lay before me.

The Other Side of Pain

The truth of the matter is this: I couldn't have identified with those people who are disregarded and broken—those people Jesus called "the least of these"—until I became one of them.

After facing the unfairness of pain and dealing with its associated losses, I began to see that there are powerful lessons we can glean from painful trials. My trials gave me a profound understanding of the other side of suffering—the instructive side.

More importantly, without my intense suffering, I might never have connected intimately with God.

Don't get me wrong. I didn't choose pain. Pain chose me. If the choice had been mine, I would have requested a more user-friendly way to learn the things I needed to learn. Who would volunteer to journey through such a traumatic and pain-filled stage of life?

I'm sure you can understand. You probably never would have chosen to go through some of the things that you have perhaps endured in your life: broken relationships; battered finances; physical and mental challenges; struggles with weight and overall health; addiction to substances or to your own compulsive habits; or feelings of loneliness, anxiety, depression and spiritual emptiness.

Most of us will live with some variation of these types of problems at some point in our lives, but that doesn't mean we can't rise above our personal catastrophes. We can free ourselves from the prisons of our mind that tell us we are doomed to despair. We can transcend our limitations to live beyond the norm.

I call that "Extraordinary Living." It's a life that each and every one of us can live, and not only those fortunate souls who are successful and pain-free.

At some point, we will walk through life with a limp in our gait that requires us to adapt, but that doesn't mean we should let our limp control our lives. Our pain doesn't mean that we need to submit to a drastically reduced concept of what life can be. There can be more to life than continually carrying the baggage of our past on the path to our future. This passion to transcend our limitations is what I mean by "Extraordinary Living."

When I was labeled "totally and permanently disabled," I felt that I had been given a life sentence of failure and futility. I accepted this medical verdict and, for a while, lived as if I was under a curse.

Extraordinary living requires that we no longer let labels determine who we are or how we live. Extraordinary living doesn't mean that we will never feel pain, but it does mean we can envision the possibility of rising above whatever ails us, of escaping whatever it is that holds us prisoner to the status quo.

How then do we muster up the power to soar beyond the physical ills and ailments that may be with us for the rest of our lives? A change in the way we think is required.

Though we may not be able to abolish our physical limitations, this does not prevent us from freely exploring the untapped power of our inner world.

Finding Your Starting Point

The transformation we must undergo to experience extraordinary living begins on the inside of us; at the core of who we are. The outer world of bodies and symptoms and contrasting voices is not where our deepest problems exist. But external calamities such as chronic illness, financial decline, excess weight or emotional depression don't need to defeat us.

Thankfully, my experience has been both internal and external. I've changed the way I think. I've changed the ways I embrace what I believe. And these changes on the inside have led to the kind of total transformation that has helped my physical ailments on the outside. I think the same can happen for you, but first, you must make a commitment to enter into a process of inner change.

Stepping Into Total Darkness

This inner change may sound appealing, but it doesn't happen easily or quickly. That's because the real estate of our inner world contains vast areas of darkness. Behind the closed doors that protect our damaged lives, fear and darkness await each one of us. You can't always see exactly what's going on behind these closed doors, but you can sure feel the chilling effects of venturing into the unknown areas of your own soul.

Our fear of the unknown is one of the biggest roadblocks preventing us from experiencing God's love and care for us. We're afraid of stepping into the unknown, particularly when the things we have done in our lives haven't turned out as well as we had hoped. We're even more afraid that God might not like what he sees in us. What then? Many of us try all the harder to hide from God, just like Adam and Eve did in the Garden after eating that apple.

God doesn't share our fear of the dark. He already knows everything there is to know about our unknown inner selves. He loves us and wants to draw nearer to us anyway! In the midst of our darkness is exactly where God meets us and—if we welcome him—takes up residence in our soul. To him, our darkness shows where the light needs to shine, and he's more than agreeable to be there with us.

Are you willing to journey deep down within yourself into that secret place where God dwells and wishes for you to enter into his presence? Stepping into the inner darkness can be horrifying, especially if you have already been shell-shocked by the trials of life. But there's no other way to experience the kind of life that lies beyond our senses. We need to invite God into our inner darkness, allowing him to bring life to an area where it seemed that life was extinct or impossible.

I never would have chosen to enter my own inner darkness, but my physical pain drove me inward. Before my disability, I fought with every ounce of breath I had against going deeper into my soul. But pain changed that. With my body turning against me, I took refuge in my soul.

The moment I took that step was the moment I began to enter into that deeper place where life-changing power operates. The moment I quit relying on my own sense of self-sufficiency was the moment I began to look to something bigger than myself for the transformation I so desperately needed.

Long story short: Starting at zero—or wherever you are—is the perfect place to begin your new journey of life.

Are you ready to quit trying to "fix yourself and step into the presence of God?"

Why Won't My Pain Go Away?

This is a simple and straightforward question, but it took me years to find the courage to ask God about my pain. Part of my reticence was due to theological doctrines that taught me my suffering should have been miraculously healed. That hadn't happened, but I didn't want to give up on my beliefs or be angry with God.

Nor did I want to be angry with the many people who have grossly misunderstood how to deal with those whose painful suffering remains incurable. Some of these church friends and business associates only made my suffering worse.

I've heard it all over the years:

"You must be sinning, so that's why God hasn't healed you."

"You should pray more if you want to be healed."

"You do not have enough faith to receive healing."

"I'll pray for you brother. Have a nice day."

"Don't think about your pain, instead, concentrate on your faith."

"Others who are suffering more than you might need God to help them first."

This is merely the short list. And I'm not alone when it comes to hearing these well-intended but unsatisfactory suggestions. In our culture, pain and suffering seem to generate little compassion. More often, these trials cause others to run as far from us as possible. And those who are running for the hills may include family members, close friends and fellow church members, who really ought to know better.

What can you do when God hasn't healed you and your friends can't comfort you?

Where do you turn when all the treatments of medical science, alternative approaches and faith-based cures have failed to bring healing?

Do you repeatedly ask for something that you're convinced won't change?

Do you ask for deliverance, even though you know the answer you want is probably not coming?

My education in the school of suffering was yielding diminishing returns. I had lived with chronic pain for more than a decade and there was no end in sight. I just couldn't see how God could love me in the midst of my pain.

No matter how much I tried to love God, and others, I experienced lowly periods when I felt totally unworthy of any love at all. I hungered for healing, but I would have settled for a sign from God directing me to the path I should take.

Pain has a way of shaking things up. Even if we think we have everything all figured out, our lives are turned inside out when pain decides to raise its powerful force.

For me, it wasn't always the burning nerve pain that spoke the loudest. There were times when the emotional pain drowned out any confidence I had about living in the present and weakened any remaining faith I had in the divine power of God within me. I was unable to see anything beyond the pain I was feeling.

During those times when I felt that every ounce of my life was being squeezed in a winepress, I often reacted emotionally. That's understandable, but my emotional reactions frustrated me because I knew that giving into my emotions is not the way one lives an extraordinary life.

But pain wasn't letting up long enough for me to figure out how to become the leader of my own destiny. Suffering pounded me profusely and unexpectedly, as sometimes happens to all of us. As I became overwhelmed, I often fell to my knees in prayer. But, more often, pain tested me and challenged me to see beyond its seeming unfairness.

During some of the bleaker times, the darkness I experienced was more than a journey into the blackness. It seemed the darkness had gained the upper hand in my life. My faith in God's love and mercy prevented me from feeling that I was utterly defeated, but I remained very fragile emotionally, and I was uncertain about how to take that next step forward.

Every time I felt like I had taken five steps forward in my spiritual growth, there were other times when it felt like I had taken ten steps backward. This spiritual-tug-of-war exhausted me and left me wondering, "How long will this continue? And how much can torment really teach me?"

Reaching Out to Get Rescued

The combination of outer and inner pain conspired to take me further and further down into despair. Like Job, the famous sufferer from the Bible, I asked God why he wouldn't rescue me from my sorrowful anguish? Isn't that his promise to all who believe in him?

Have you ever been in a place like this? Have you ever felt a similar despair during those times when life seems overwhelming? Where do you go? What do you do next when you can't see any way out of your own miseries, regardless of how they came to be?

I believed that God already knew everything about me, my pain, and my thoughts, regardless of how far he seemed from me. I knew there was no place I could hide from him to find relief from my circumstances. Candidly, I guess you could say I reached the point where I didn't care anymore.

That was when I finally got totally real. I had finally been stripped bare. I was powerless without the armor I had used to cover the wounds of my soul. I had no more back-up plans. I no longer had the energy to "stuff" my emotions or hide my real feelings from God.

Again and again, I poured out my complaint and asked God, *"Why won't my pain go away?"*

I wasn't the first person in history to raise the pain question. Listen to what the prophet Jeremiah said thousands of years earlier:

> *Why is my pain unceasing,*
> *my wound incurable,*
> *refusing to be healed?*
> *Will you be to me like a deceitful brook,*
> *like waters that fail?*
> (Jeremiah 15:18, all scriptures from
> the *English Standard Version Bible*).

Perhaps the Lord would respond to me as he had to Jeremiah's inquiry:

> *Therefore thus says the Lord:*
> *"If you return, I will restore you"*
> (Jeremiah 15:19a).

What did it mean to return to God? I wasn't aware of ever leaving him.

Initially, I felt I didn't get the response I was hoping for. In fact, I didn't hear anything at all from God. I didn't hear the whispers of his Spirit within me. I didn't sense his urgings in the dark places of my heart. I didn't immediately extrapolate any deeper meanings from the Word. Nor did anyone apprise me about God's answer to my poignant question.

Dead silence is what I was left with for quite some time.

From Theory to Practice

I hope the lessons I have learned on my journey might help you on yours. To help you convert my ideas into actions that will work for you, I will close each chapter with some practical suggestions. Here are some of the key life insights from this chapter:

Insights for the Journey

- Take it easy. Don't be too hard on yourself. We all suffer losses in life. Don't add to your problems by indulging in self-rejection. This negative self-talk hinders your ability to become an overcomer.
- Don't expect everything to change overnight. Change takes time, and better living often happens in the midst of physical, emotional and spiritual pain.
- Be willing to confront your fears to step into the dark places of your soul to discover the life-giving light of God.
- Let go. Don't try to run the universe. Pain makes people want to take control, but you have no control over God's love and power.

• •

Two

Making Peace with Your Pain

Pain is the body's natural response to injury. When you're a child and you place your hand on a hot burner, your body tells you: "Hey, this hurts! Get away from that burner, and don't do this anymore!"

The lessons we learn about pain in childhood stick with us the rest of our lives, and whether we suffer from physical pain or pain of the soul, we try to avoid it whenever possible.

Most of the time it makes sense to run in the opposite direction when you encounter pain. And when the pain is chronic, you want to run as far and as fast as you can. But in this chapter, I want to ask you to consider a different approach for dealing with the various kinds of pain we experience in life. I am going to ask you to embrace your pain and step through it to something better.

Embracing your pain may sound counter-intuitive. It may even sound crazy. But, I can tell you this: It works!

Let me explain what I mean.

Confronting CRPS

It was 1997 and I had reached the end of the road. I had contracted an aggressive neuropathic condition known as CRPS, which stands for Complex Regional Pain Syndrome.

CRPS is a terrifying condition in which the body's normal sympathetic nerve reactions turn into hyper-exaggerated responses. Even the lightest forms of touch, pressure and temperature can cause excruciating pain.

I was not able to differentiate between hot or cold, nor was I able to tolerate any type of sensation against my skin. Wearing clothes was out of the question. Trying to bathe myself was virtually impossible. From the time I woke up in the morning to the time I finally fell asleep at night, it felt as if there was a lit match touching the tender parts of my swollen flesh. As a result, I lived life naked, crying, sleep-deprived and writhing in agony without relief. It was an awful time.

I underwent practically every treatment imaginable to reduce the pain, including medical, alternative and faith-based methods. All kinds of narcotic drugs were administered, as my pain management team experimented with different dosages and a variety of cocktail mixtures to try getting my condition under control.

Regardless of their approaches, the high-powered medications barely helped to reduce the intensity of my torment.
As a result, my prognosis was very poor. In fact, it was dire.
The possibility of death seemed to be tormenting me in the
darkest core of my inner being.

I had reached an endpoint: a place of utter hopelessness
where there was no conceivable option for making things
any better. I was frightened to try anything new out of fear
that any other treatments would only make things worse
than they already were. And, even though I still believed in
God, my faith didn't seem to make any concrete contribu-
tions to improving my situation. I knew God loved me, but
that didn't take away my pain.

I didn't realize it at the time, but I was not alone. Many
people find themselves trapped within destructive and repet-
itive patterns of irresolvable pain, leading them to feelings of
hopelessness. When we're in this place, our minds go around
and around, worrying about the things we can't resolve and
frustrated that we're really not headed anywhere in life. No
matter how much we struggle to break free from our physical and emotional challenges, it's easier to stay stuck in that
place where we feel completely defeated by our suffering.

Have you ever reached such an endpoint? A place in life
where your problems appear unending and your life continues to unravel as time marches onward? A place where
the progress of time is *not* a healer, but only the minute-by-
minute record of your unsuccessful battle with anguish? A

place where you're unsure if it's worth continuing to run the race of life?

I had certainly reached my endpoint. And it was only then that I realized an endpoint could also be a starting point. Whenever a person is beat down and desperate, a new opportunity can beckon.

The new opportunity I had was to have a different response to my own pain. I had tried to run from it, medicate it, and ignore it. What if I embraced it?

That's what I did. Instead of avoiding my pain as I had done since I was a child encountering a hot burner, I moved toward it, approaching it like a long lost friend. Instead of running away from pain as best as I could, I stepped toward it.

Instead of hiding and cowering in the shadow of my pain, I confronted it. Rather than being immobilized by fear, I boldly stepped into the darkest places of my soul. Instead of ignoring the ever-present torment of my own physical and emotional brokenness, I connected on a deeper level with my own wounds.

Each step I took forward, toward my pain, was a step into the unknown. I felt like an explorer in the deepest, darkest expanse of the Amazon jungle. I didn't know if I would emerge alive or be lost forever in the encompassing darkness. But, I continued, step by step. The closer I got to the heart of my pain, the more every part of my being protested and resisted my progress.

FACING & EMBRACING OUR PAIN

I didn't know what I would find, but I knew that something was already changing within me. Instead of allowing myself to be victimized by my own pain, I was taking active steps to confront it.

The further I traveled toward embracing my pain, the more I began to see my brokenness from a new and refreshing perspective. I got a closer look at the walls I had erected to keep myself safe from my pain and from pain from others. I started seeing the many false images I had created about my purpose in life - and, who I was.

I also saw that my pain and many physical problems required spiritual solutions, not the habitual patterns of avoidance I had developed over the years. And for the first time on my journey, the darkness started to give way to the light. In the wreckage of my own brokenness I could detect the light of a new life awaiting me.

As I progressed deeper into my soul, I began to loosen the tight grip I had on my own thoughts regarding my need to control every area in my life. The more I let go, the more strength I felt I had to pursue the spiritual side of living. The more I loosened up my grip on my own pain and suffering, the more I felt that I was learning to free myself from the power that my pain and weakness held over me.

A Journey of a Million Steps

I wish I could tell you that everything suddenly became perfect once I began this journey to embrace my pain. But, patterns of behavior that we have followed for a lifetime don't vanish overnight. Nor can we immediately shed the instinctual reactions we have to protect ourselves from pain.

Instead, a journey of transformation is just that: a journey. If you embark on a one-mile walk or a hike, you will need to take some 2,000 steps to reach your goal. But journeys inward require more time and dedication to complete, and often continue for much longer than we ever anticipate. In part, that's because when we embark on an inner journey, we're not simply traveling from Point A to Point B. We're going wherever the road takes us, and usually that means following twists and turns to areas of our soul that we never knew existed.

The journey inward is a unique and personal journey to the heart of who we truly are. There's no one-size-fits-all map that we can follow on this inward journey, because we're all different. From the wiring of our brain circuitry to the idiosyncrasies of our individual souls, we are all created differently and have our own unique responses to the challenges of life. The one thing we have in common is that we are searching for happiness in a big, busy and often troublesome world.

I've learned much about the search for happiness from watching children, who have wonderful instincts about how to live. It seems children are drawn to those who laugh; to those who choose to have more fun; to those who choose innocence; to those who choose to show love instead of those who exhibit destructive behaviors, such as anger, hostility, jealously and dissension.

Don't we want the same things that children long for? Don't we want to possess the treasures that make our hearts sparkle with joy?

The reality is that none of us have a clean and perfect heart. We may long for childlike innocence, but we have become broken and discouraged. So what do we do when we can no longer endure our damaged lives? How you answer this question reveals whether your brokenness has overtaken your life and rendered you incapable of seeking change.

How do you want to live out the rest of your life? Will you suffer as a lifetime prisoner to your own misery, or will you start the journey to a new life with one first step, then another, and another?

Each of us has but two choices: to remain embittered to our painful losses or to embrace our afflictions with open arms and seek to transcend them. That's the choice we face, no matter how much these might have hurt us or how unfairly we've been mistreated.

CHOSING TO CHANGE

Broken People in a Broken World

Wherever you look today you can see people struggling with their own brokenness.

That's certainly true in the case of physical brokenness. Studies show that one out of four Americans struggle with chronic pain. That's nearly 80 million people. In addition, half the people with cancer say they battle chronic pain.

Obesity rates are also growing. Approximately one-third of Americans are obese. You would think statistics like this would encourage people to be more proactive about implementing proper ways of eating and exercising, but few seem to take the warnings seriously. As a result, there are also increases in other harmful conditions, such as diabetes, heart disease and cancer, which are occurring at astonishingly higher rates.

Other signs of our brokenness as human beings can be seen in our frequent divorces, drug addictions, wars, crimes, and suicides. In the last few years, our brokenness has even been reflected in our battered economy, which has thrown many into unemployment and homelessness.

Some people look around at our broken world and are inspired to change things for the better. These are bright lights in the darkness.

But, many of us become overwhelmed and desensitized by the sadness all around. When we see news reports about wars, crimes, murders, military atrocities, earthquakes, fires, hurricanes, tornadoes or nuclear meltdowns, we watch silently on television but basically do nothing to make things better. We let all this negative information stuff our heads, but then we try going about our business as if nothing is wrong.

A David and Goliath Battle

You may remember the story of David and Goliath from your Sunday school lessons. David was a teenager from ancient Israel who volunteered to fight Goliath, a huge and deadly Philistine warrior. The odds were certainly stacked against David, whose weapon was a simple slingshot and five smooth stones. If you remember the story, you know that God helped David knock out Goliath with a stone from his slingshot.

Did David know he would be victorious? We're not sure what his frame of mind was. But he went out to do battle with Goliath anyway. That's one of the powerful lessons of this story. Another important lesson is that God often helps us when we choose to do the right thing.

You may not be fighting a literal giant, but does it ever seem like you are battling forces bigger than yourself? The important thing when you find yourself facing difficult odds is to determine how you will respond to your seemingly unmanageable situation.

Although you may have shown tremendous resiliency at certain times, and you might have brilliantly demonstrated the power of the human spirit during episodes of overpowering opposition, it takes more than mortal power to achieve victory over the monstrosities we constantly encounter.

Oftentimes, the most unmanageable parts of our lives bring us opportunities to grow in our trust of God, to create new vision for living and to walk on a new path of living—one that moves us closer to the core of who we really are.

These were the kinds of opportunities I was given in my battles against CRPS. These battles involved periods of hospitalization as well as sympathetic blockades, which involve inserting a needle into the spinal cord and injecting a powerful anesthesia similar to the drugs that are given to expectant mothers who are about to deliver. The blockades caused complete loss of sensation to the most painful areas. For me, the experience was similar to having my nervous system "shut down" from my chest downward.

These treatments failed to quell my physical pain, and they did even less to mend the deeper brokenness within. When I finally reached my endpoint, I experienced mixed emotions. On one hand, I felt completely defeated by pain and the dramatic losses. On the other, I sensed I was being given an opportunity to really connect with God on a deeper level than I had ever known before.

What did I have to lose except the life I had once tried to create? And what did I stand to gain, other than becoming whole and experiencing the fullness of what life really means?

At times, I felt like David confronting the Goliath of CRPS. It seemed ridiculous to ask God for his divine assistance, especially since I had largely brushed aside my faith when the pain wouldn't quit.

In the end, David hadn't really been stronger than Goliath, nor was I mightier than CRPS. But what I find remarkable about David is that he never questioned the faithfulness of God, no matter how large his enemies were.

During my times of doubting God, he never scolded me or turned his back on me. Instead, he allowed me to reach the end of my own strength until I turned, once again, to him for help and deliverance. Like David fighting Goliath, I would not need to fight alone, but would have God fighting alongside me.

Owning Our Brokenness

I remained captive to my pain and brokenness until I gave up! Everything changed once I quit trying to hide from my problems, began embracing them, and sought to overcome them with the loving faithfulness of God.

I believe the same holds true for all of us. We will remain captive to our brokenness as long as we try to maintain a tight control over every area of our lives. But there's great freedom and power to be found in letting go, especially when we feel like we're imprisoned in a valley of indecision and hopelessness.

We will continue to struggle against super-sized enemies even when we place our trust in God. Again, the key is to let go, allowing his strength to bind up our weakness so that we can be like David confronting Goliath.

Trusting God with our battles is not something that comes naturally for us here in the land of the free and home of the brave. Instead, we prefer to tackle our problems on our own, embracing an ethos of rugged individualism much like John Wayne embraced when attacking his enemies.

But, I knew I couldn't face my giants on my own. That made it easier for me to rely on God's grace and guidance. What that meant for me was simple. I had to embrace and ultimately *forgive* what I completely loathed; CRPS and its unrelenting pain, and the ways it had stripped me of my identity, security, sense of well-being and purpose.

Forgive my pain? Yes. I have found that the most effective way to fight a large and destructive enemy is to forgive it. In fact, forgiveness is one of the most powerful weapons we have in this life, whether it be forgiving people with whom we have been in relationship or other things and thoughts and systems that torment us and embitter our hearts.

Embracing your brokenness means to step into the darker places of pain with an attitude of forgiveness.

When my pain was too much for me, I really didn't have the power within myself to forgive those things that kept violently hurting me. Instead, I found the power of forgiveness through the Spirit of God. By opening my own heart to the work of God's Spirit, I allowed his power to seep into the dark and broken places in my life. Trusting God was a significant exercise of faith on my part. But that's the thing about trust. It requires our complete surrender. In this case, I was willing to open myself to his transforming power that is much bigger than me and my relatively little problems.

Rather than trying to have dominion over everything through our own power, forgiveness teaches us that there are hidden aspects to life that are known and controlled only by God. In the light of God's forgiveness, we can begin to see how our suffering and pain are ultimately part of a bigger and better purpose.

Forgiveness frees us from the grip of the enemy—whatever that enemy is. Forgiveness allows a transfer of power to occur deep within us, and this transfer from our David-sized power to God's Goliath-sized power loosens the hold that brokenness has in our lives. Instead of brokenness reigning over us and every aspect of our lives, a dynamic shift occurs within the deeper recesses of our soul.

Forgiveness gives each and every one of us the key to our prisons. Forgiveness frees us to unlock the doors of our cell and to walk freely into a renewing way of life.

THE POWER OF FORGIVENESS

In the case of my battle against the pain of CRPS, forgiveness meant that I could place my pain and burdens in the darkest place of human suffering, at the foot of the cross of Christ. The more I let go of my own pain, the more I gained strength to carry onward another day. The more strength I gained inwardly, the less I was controlled by the physical pain of CRPS, even though its nastiness persisted for quite some time. In essence, I grew in compassion toward life despite what I had to suffer. And, ultimately, forgiveness offered one of its valuable gifts of freedom to me. I didn't have to carry around any more thoughts of guilt about my deficiencies and what I was going through.

Eventually, my CRPS went into remission. And though I still live with chronic pain, dealing with this thorn in my flesh has given me a much deeper connection with God. It has opened my eyes to the fact that we all share in the brokenness of the human condition. This has given me clearer vision in my quest for the real treasures of life.

Making Peace with Pain

Are you ready to make peace with your pain? Are you willing to embrace your pain and brokenness so that you can forgive them and experience freedom from their control over your life? Can you stop living on your own strength so that God can give you his strength to fight your battles? Are you ready to begin life again? Have you reached the place where you're finally ready to experience a different and better way of living, despite your brokenness?

If so, I welcome you to the journey. All you need to do is take that first step toward your pain and God's love. And another. Then another. Then another.

Insights for the Journey

- Take that heroic step into your pain. Stop battling your painful losses with your own might. You will discover how your physical catastrophes are also linked to who you are spiritually.
- Stop trying to completely control your life and attempting to solve the world's problems on your own. Seek truth and bask in its redeeming power.
- Embrace your afflictions with open arms of forgiveness, no matter how much these afflictions have hurt you or how unfairly you've been treated. Take the path of God's grace instead of the path of rugged individualism.
- Learn how to own your brokenness. Although it's an individual process, it carries the transforming power of God. Draw closer to God in your pain. Let him set you free from your miseries.

Three

• • •

The Moment of Truth

It can happen to any one of us at any time, but it seems to happen when we least expect it. It's a moment of truth—that instant when the blinders seem to fall from our eyes and we can see reality as it is, in all its rawness.

Perhaps you have experienced moments in which you can suddenly see new aspects of your life, or your relationships, or issues in your career. These flashes of insight are unique to each one of us, since they uncover hidden aspects of who we truly are. These momentary epiphanies don't come with an owner's manual that explains what to do. They simply arrive, challenging our assumptions and habits while presenting us with the opportunity to make a fresh assessment of what's real and what's not.

Have you ever experienced one of these moments of truth, when everything around you seemed insignificant compared to the power and clarity of that soul-shaking moment? When the sense of truthfulness and honesty spoke to your inner being more loudly than the many other voices you've listened to before?

These are important questions, because moments of truth are one of life's precious gifts. They come to us freely, but they demand our attention. Will we accept new insights that confront our old, established ways of seeing things? And more importantly, will we change the ways we live our life to incorporate these revelations of truth?

My Morning Moment

One significant moment of truth happened early one hot Tuesday morning in the summer of 2006. It was noticeable in part because my life had become a dull, robotic drill.

I had been dealing with Complex Regional Pain Syndrome (CRPS) for nearly a decade, but I still lived with pronounced levels of chronic pain. As a result, my days were mostly generic and stagnant. I followed a conservative routine to ensure that I didn't injure myself further. Although I was working part-time and contributing to the life of my family, I really felt like I was dying inside.

My typical day followed a predictable pattern: Eat breakfast. Shower. Get dressed. Read and pray. Then I would head to the office—no matter how tired and defeated I emotionally felt—where I would focus all the energy I could muster on enduring the hectic schedule that each and every day had in store for me.

Like many people whose days become anchored to such a predictable pattern, I regularly experienced a sense of disappointment and purposelessness that often resulted in heart-stabbing bitterness and even despair. I felt like I had so much potential and there was so much I could offer the world, but my potential wasn't being used. Subsequently, I felt unnecessary and unfulfilled.

In time, I had given up on living an abundant life and focused instead on merely existing, which isn't really living at all. I was primarily occupied with trying to control my pain, but this narrow focus effectively prevented me from fully using the gifts that God had given me.

As I crawled out of bed that Tuesday morning in 2006 after fighting through another sleepless night, I had no idea that anything unusual would alter my dull, daily pattern. After I gulped down a nondescript breakfast, I sought refuge in the shower, standing with my back to the stream of hot water for an inordinate amount of time, hoping to purge the fatigue from my mind and body.

But the shower hadn't washed away my gloom. If anything, I was more exhausted than usual, and I didn't have an ounce of energy to carry on. I was fed up with my existence, and felt that I had reached the end of my rope.

I stepped out of the shower and wrapped myself in a large towel. Next I went to the mirror to begin making myself presentable for another day.

That's when my moment of truth happened.

As I stood there looking at my big, soaking wet, body, I was aghast. The person I saw gazing back at me looked like a complete stranger. I couldn't believe what I saw. I knew that I had become overweight because of my years of medication use, physical inactivity and dietary neglect. Being overweight is one thing, but as I looked at myself in the mirror I realized that I had suddenly become unmanageably obese.

"Who is this big, fat pig looking at me through bloodshot eyes buried in puffy cheeks?" I muttered to myself.

Reluctantly, I let my towel drop to the floor so I could take in the whole scene. For years when I looked at myself in the mirror, I hadn't really seen things clearly. Now, in my moment of truth, I could see myself for who I had really become. Now, for the first time in ages, I carefully examined every inch of my body, above and below the neckline. It wasn't a pretty sight.

"What have I done to myself!" was all I could think.

Making the Moment Last

There's an interesting thing about moments of truth. We can't make them happen or control when they come to us. All we can control is how we will respond to them. Like any gift, these moments can be received with open arms or they can be rejected. The choice is completely yours.

I don't know why, but that Tuesday morning I decided to welcome my moment of truth and follow it as far as it would take me. Without really thinking about what I was doing, I heard myself speaking honestly, saying things I might have thought before, but had never expressed out loud.

"Gordon," I said, addressing myself in the mirror. "What have you done to yourself? You must be an idiot!"

I intently kept staring at my flabby, damaged body. Myriad questions and random thoughts came to mind.

"How is this body a testimony of God's grace at work in your life?"

"I must look like the biggest hypocrite in the world."

"Am I too far gone to ever recapture what I had apparently lost - any hope of better health and a better life?"

Then I turned my attention away from myself and toward something bigger.

"God," I cried out, in a weak, faltering voice. "Here I am. I'm ugly. I'm fat. I haven't treated my body as a holy temple. I haven't lived the life I should have lived. Like King David, I have sinned against you. I have been living a life of self-delusion."

The more I confessed to God, the longer my moment of truth seemed to last, and the more I had to say.

"I am standing literally naked before you, God," I said. "I have no towel to hide behind. I stand ashamed. I am totally

THE MOMENT OF TRUTH

embarrassed about who I've become. I truly don't know who I am. I don't even know if I can make it another day like this, and I'm not really sure I have any more energy to try to make things better."

My hopeless confession continued until I ran out of negative things to say about myself, then I reached beyond myself in humble prayer.

"God, I need you. I'm asking you for help. I am asking to be changed, healed and transformed."

I wish I could say that a bolt of lightning arced across the mirror and that a band of heavenly angels came to serenade me. But nothing like that happened. I wasn't watching a super-spectacular, digitally enhanced movie.

Instead, something more lasting and profound occurred. I took in a deep breath. And with that breath came in something I hadn't experienced in a long, long time. I tasted hope.

A Poor Man's Pride

Isn't it uncanny that even the most desperate and broken person can be proud and stubborn? It seems that even when we are stuck within the mire of our doldrums, we stubbornly grasp and cling to our condition rather than allow it to be transformed into something better.

That's because our brokenness can lead to a form of pride that actively creates lies—lies of denial that not only separate us from the truth but also hinder truth's transforming power.

Instead of seeking inner transformation, we double down and work harder on trying to correct our external problems. But, hard work will not erase life's disappointments or remedy the brokenness within our hearts. The same is true of good works. Endlessly doing good things will not eradicate the guilt we feel about not living up to the amazing potential that all of us possess. Trying to make up for the losses doesn't wipe the slate of our hearts clean to begin afresh.

Not even religious practices are enough to erase our heartaches and disappointments. For centuries, disciples of various religions have practiced forms of penance, which involve burdensome punishments for wrongful living. But self-punishment doesn't yield the kind of grace we need to depend upon God for his tender mercies and his delivering power to transform the human spirit.

I had tried so many of these imperfect approaches, but when my morning moment of truth arrived, I realized that my pride did not provide me with any covering to hide behind. Like Adam and Eve in the Garden of Eden, I had been found out. I could either choose to engage in another cycle of self-denial or I could choose to allow this moment to be an opportunity to start my life on a new course.

For years, I had chosen to take pride in my suffering and trust in myself rather than entirely trusting in God's healing love. Sure, I was a person of much faith, and during some painful trials, I had experienced significant spurts of spiritual growth. But in truth, I wasn't giving myself *fully* to God.

That's because I didn't know what it meant or how it felt to completely trust God. Instead, I created my own secure place deep within myself where I felt safe and protected against the fear and anguish that were my daily realities.

For me, self-protection was the path of least resistance. That's understandable. Whenever we are incapacitated by pain or loss, it's easy to respond by burrowing deeper within ourselves and hiding from the painful realities outside.

As parts of me were dying day by day, I responded by clinging more tenaciously to those few things I still had, relying more thoroughly on self-protection to guard against anything that might cause additional pain or hardship. Yet, my attempts to shield myself from further hurts simply fostered these addictions that I later discovered, included compulsive eating, lavish spending, prolonged laziness and relentless self-criticism.

During my moment of truth, I saw that I was doing the very things I despised. I had swallowed the lie at the root of human sinfulness. I had unwittingly become consumed by pride.

The Powerlessness of Penance

For years, I had tried to justify my disappointing life to God and persuade him to like me through my performance of religious deeds. For me, these religious acts were a form of penance, or self-punishment. And these religious self-efforts kept me in a state of denial, within which I couldn't recognize who I truly was in all of my fatness.

I was reading the Bible over and over again in several different translations and versions. I was industriously studying inspirational and theological books, praying endless hours, fasting for truth, working with and financially supporting worthwhile ministries, and regularly attending church services and prayer meetings. There were times when I believed that such acts were helping me to rise above other tortured souls who, like me, were trying to climb the ladder of spiritual approval and success. But these many practices failed to achieve the two things I desired most.

First, I wasn't getting any closer to God, though I did experience infrequent moments of intimacy with his Spirit.

Second, I hadn't experienced God's healing touch. The New Testament is full of stories of people who were miraculously healed by the touch of Jesus, but these stories seemed far removed from my relentless pain and despair.

I felt more like Jeremiah, the Old Testament prophet, who asked, *"Why is my pain unceasing, my wound incurable, refusing to be healed"* (Jeremiah 15:18a).

Many religious and spiritual people try inflicting their own forms of strict penance on themselves, believing they can justify themselves to God through various acts of self-deprivation, hoping that these deeds will atone for their wrongdoing and allow them to live out their faith more effectively. Yet, what tends to actually happen is that penance confirms our distance from God and imprisons us in our own miseries. That's because penance can be a form of pride. We embrace penance because we think it will help us cover up our sense of self-pity. Instead, it blinds us to the truth of God. And when we realize that our penance has failed to make our lives any better, we doubt God, questioning his faithfulness and his ability to heal the atrocities of human suffering.

In our pride, we put God on trial for the failings of humanity in a sin-filled world. Meanwhile, we justify ourselves by investing more deeply in our pride and self-protection.

In the long run, seeking to justify ourselves through religious acts will not put us on a new path for better living. Our new journey requires something beyond feeble human efforts to make things better.

Are you ready to let go of your pride and self-protection so you can consider a different way? If so, take a deep breath and get ready to experience the same thing I experienced during my morning moment of truth: *hope*.

From Penance to Repentance

What comes to mind when you hear the word repentance? The two words—penance and repentance—sound similar, and they are often confused. But they couldn't be more different.

I had mistakenly confused repentance with other religious terms involving forms of faith that were strict and legalistic.

Frankly, I didn't see any value in adding another religious custom to my routines. Plus, why should I repent and confess my sins when I already felt low enough? I felt like I had earned the equivalent of a doctorate degree from the seminary of suffering where the lessons of humility were being instilled daily. Why would I need to practice repentance? What additional value was there in the confession of sin when I was already atoned by the loving grace of Jesus Christ?

I know I am not alone in asking these questions. When you're feeling colossal-sized pain, and you're trying to cope with unworkable obstacles, and you're stuck in the worst living conditions of your life, the last thing you want to do is to make yourself more vulnerable, become weaker, or be ridiculed about where your life has ended up. No one needs to tell you how bad things are in your life, and on the flip side, it's highly unlikely that you feel like sharing your banal existence with anyone else anyway.

This is when change seems impossible for you.

Thankfully, I have since come to view penance and repentance differently. For me, penance is essentially punitive. It uses works and deeds to seek justification and make amends for the penalties of foolish choices.

Repentance, on the other hand, is an instrument of divine grace. Properly expressed, it is an ongoing process of confession that helps us die to ourselves so we then can live for God.

I know I have grown closer to God through confessing my failures and brokenness to him. Regular repentance has also allowed me to view myself more honestly, as well as express myself more intimately with God through his Spirit. The truth is that repentance is not about self-punishment and godly deeds. Rather, it's about emptying yourself. This creates an opening for God's grace and the sanctifying work of his Spirit to empower your steps in the journey of life.

When a person exchanges penance and self-protection for repentance and complete openness to God, authentic change becomes possible.

I didn't really understand this during my morning moment of truth. Instead, it seemed like God was not listening to my pleas for help, at least not the way I was asking for help. The idea of God's forgiving power seemed like a cruel joke—a mirage of water in a life that felt like a desert of suffering. I was operating from a position of doubt, not faith, as I stared into the mirror, unable to recognize the person looking back at me.

But when hope entered my desert of despair that morning, it felt like I had been given a cup of cool, clear water. I felt like I had been crawling on my hands and knees, and was offered a drink from the cup of repentance.

Unlike the self-punishment of penance - true repentance helps to stimulate growth from the inside-out of our entire being. It assists us in our pursuit of self-discovery by tearing down the walls of our self-justifying tendencies. Instead of relying on our own limited power to create a process of change, repentance connects us with the power of God and his infinite possibilities for change in our lives.

Returning to Life

Many people say they want change in their lives, but are they willing to let go of the self-protective practices they have clung to in the past?

I sought change for years, or at least I thought I had. But in order to experience true transformation, I had to be *willing* to change, before transformation would even be possible. I also knew I needed to be fully honest with God, worshipping him in spirit and truth and humility as I sought to walk on a new path.

In many ways, the process of life-change is like a jet plane lifting off the ground. How does an aircraft weighing a million or more pounds rise into the air against the laws of physics and gravity? Initially, the process of flight is very difficult. Movement in the right direction seems slow going. But as the plane builds up speed on the runway, you can sense the battle between the natural forces of gravity and the anticipated lift-off from the ground into the wide-open blue skies. Before long, you and hundreds of other passengers are soaring tens of thousands of feet above the earth.

Life-change happens in a similar way. Before we take off we must be willing to break free from our bewildered lives and journey into newer and better ways of living. Although sin and brokenness still exist and try to keep us grounded in the same ruts, their hold over us is not absolute. We can break free from these attachments, much as a plane overcomes the persistent power of gravity.

That's what true repentance does for those of us who believe. It turns our lives around, reorienting us in the right direction and moving us toward God. Repentance empowers us to walk on a new path of living by helping us to break free from the dynamics of sin working against us.

Where I once believed it to be confining, repentance is truly liberating. It peels away the dying layers of our old habits and our self-defenses so that our souls can begin to soar above the gravitational pull of our past failures and self doubts.

The process was painful. I had to let go of long-held views about who I was, what I wanted to be and how I wanted to be acknowledged by others. These old notions were completely torn down so I could finally see who I really was. Confessing my worries, my pain, my false sense of self-importance, my disappointments, my sin, my junk and everything else to God, opened my spiritual eyes to see myself for how God saw me.

I began to see beyond my pain, my flab, my pride, as well as my fear. I developed an inner confidence in the faithfulness of God to bring me out of my depressed emotions and destructive thoughts. This gave birth to a profound hope that healed me and transformed me, remaking me according to God's purpose for me. In essence, returning to God was like returning to life.

The Choice Is Yours

The same kind of transformation is available to you. The choice is yours. It's part of your free will to take that *first* step toward God. Once you do so, you are in a position to receive the promise that he will then draw near to you (James 4:8).

Does this seem hard to imagine? Then I challenge you to envision a life that you probably can't imagine yet - a life in which you break free from your encumbrances to experience the freedom of being airborne - a life of day-by-day, moment-by-moment transformation.

Please don't wait to begin (or continue) the exciting process of change. Let's keep on our journey of transformation together and see what's next in this beautiful undertaking.

Insights for the Journey

- Your moment of truth happens when you're completely honest about who you are and your relationship with God. Truth stands on its own power. It doesn't require popular support. And, it is not overcome by your harmful choices.

- It's very easy to fall into the trap of trying to make yourself "right" through various religious practices. Resist self-condemnation. Don't put God on trial for your painful losses. Instead, open yourself up fully and be vulnerable with him.

- It's impossible to guarantee permanent changes for your life without God. Put your pride aside. Confess your sin and repent. Be open and honest with God, learning how to communicate with the intimacy of his Spirit. Truth helps you to accept the reality of your circumstances.

- You must be humble to change. Confession and repentance will help you to draw near to God, and he will then draw closer to you. Imagine the possibilities for your life after this divine connection becomes re-established!

Four

. . . .

Overcoming Doubt

There I was, fresh from my bathroom mirror epiphany and ready to get on with my new life. After seeing my situation in a revealing light, I was determined to make some significant changes in the way I did things.

But before I could take even one step forward, I was ambushed by a most treacherous enemy: doubt.

Doubt can steal our dreams and demolish our beliefs. This enemy seems especially powerful whenever we're trying to make changes for the better. At these moments of hope, doubt sows uncertainty and can demoralize us.

Doubt is so destructive because it plays on the way our brains and hearts are wired. It acts as one of our primal survival mechanisms, but we don't need to let it rule our lives. In the following pages I want to help you overcome the death-grip that doubt may have on your own mind and heart.

Lost On the Neurological Highway

Brains are powerful processors. Unfortunately, the way our brains are wired can also cause us to remain stuck in unhealthy behaviors.

Our brains process the information gathered through our senses (seeing, hearing, smelling, tasting and touching). As the brain processes this constant flow of information, these neurological impulses create pathways in the brain. Neuroscientists believe that these pathways create patterns that influence the ways our brain will process information in the future.

Think of neurological pathways as a railroad system in our brains. Thoughts travel from here to there like trains down a set of railroad tracks. Trains can change tracks with some effort if engineers make them do so, but most of the time they are simply required to travel down the same set of tracks they commonly traverse.

In the same way, our brains have familiar, well-traveled routes. That's OK until we want to change our lives. Intuitively, our brains want to voyage down the most familiar tracks. What that means in practice is that efforts to change our lives will be met by protests from the brain that want to protect our familiar routines of doing things. In other words, our brain, which prefers the status quo, sends out the mental patterns to follow, and usually, that's exactly what we do. We follow.

You can't be a follower if you want to change your life. You need to be a leader. You need to have a grown-up talk with your brain, which may include recalling painful trials from the past. You need to alert your internal processor that there's something new being built in your life, and that requires the construction of some new neural pathways.

Otherwise, your brain will send the same signals along the same pathways it has traveled before. When that happens, you can become stuck in a holding pattern, weighed down by life's problems. You already have enough challenges trying to break free from old patterns or addictive behaviors. You don't need to make things harder by being sideswiped by your own brain.

Doubt thrives when your life is in a holding pattern. That's why doubt doesn't want us to build any new railroad tracks in our brains. Instead, it wants to keep us traveling down the familiar neurological pathways of the past, so it tries to sabotage our hopes, and strangles our beliefs about the possibility of a better tomorrow. It blinds our eyes to new visions. It makes us afraid to boldly explore new territories.

The good news is that you can change your life if you are also willing to pay attention to the way your brain processes information. You can't break away from old addictions or reform old ways of handling negative experiences without radically changing the neurological railroad tracks in your brain.

In fact, the common "cold turkey" approach many people take toward breaking old addictions is really a misnomer. There's more to moving forward than merely trying to withdraw from your unhealthy habits. If you really want to see transformation take place in your life you will also need to create new, healthier habits, and integrate these into your life and consciously retrain your brain.

Are you ready to get to work and lay down some new railroad tracks in your brain? Are you willing to break with the past by trying new behaviors and attitudes? Can you incorporate healthy changes into a new view of how you will live your life?

If you're willing to forge ahead with these changes in your life, you will be able to protect yourself from the enemy of doubt that tries to destroy your plans for the future.

From Vision to Action

During and after my bathroom mirror epiphany, my mind received new visions (or concepts, or ideas) for the ways I could change my life. Visions come and go, but they leave each of us with an important question: How should I act on them? Should I act on all these new ideas I have for making changes? Or should I focus on the ideas that seem most powerful and act only on them?

My experience has been that the more I try to rationally assess what I'm actually going to do with the new visions for my life, the more these visions pass away. I am afraid that in this process I have unintentionally dismissed visions that could have had a powerful impact on my life. I think all of us have sloughed off some pretty good ideas over the span of our lives.

As doubts tried to attack my bathroom mirror experience, I defended it. This was *not* just an ordinary occurrence. The visions I saw for my future were *not* just a series of random thoughts. On the contrary, I believed I had been given divine insights for breaking the hardness of my heart and healing the pain and disappointment I had experienced over the years. I believed the visions I received could help tear down the prideful lies I had hidden behind, and open my mind and emotions to the voice of God's Spirit.

The battle in my mind continued the rest of the day. These doubts assailed my visions. Meanwhile, my hopes for a better future clung to the visions as a viable way I could move forward.

At some point in the battle, I decided to quit debating and start doing. I began moving from reflection to action. That decisiveness made all the difference for me, and I believe action is essential for you as well.

Seeing new visions for the future is fun and exciting. But when the visions end, actions must begin. That's why I decided that the next day would be application day. This would be the time that I would move from being stuck in a state of doubt and bondage toward navigating a new path for my life with this newly gained vision.

None of us can erase nor can we revise our past. What we can change is the future. We can accomplish great things if we have the willingness to make different choices. A new vision can present us with a new range of choices in our lives. But change won't happen until we make the hard choices required and embrace them as the new direction for our future. New choices help us avoid repeating our same old patterns.

So, when does the process move from vision to action? As soon as you choose to put the new vision into action. The practical action of change begins the very second you believe it can actually happen. The process of being transformed begins here and now. It starts when you make prudent and positive choices that put you on your new path of living.

Visions are great, but it's the day after receiving a vision that we are tested in our desire and commitment to transformation. Your doubts will be telling you to question your new vision and to just go on with your life as normal. This is when you need to double down and start fighting for the potential you have seen. Your new vision for living is a gift. Now it's your turn to follow through on the hunger for change that's been rumbling in your soul.

Changing the Things You Can Change

Doubt continues to battle you as you chart a new path into the future, opposing every effort toward putting your vision into action. It seems that the more positive steps you take, the more the battle for your new life intensifies.

As I worked to put my new vision for living into action, I drew both inspiration and practical help from the principles found in the "Serenity Prayer" from Reinhold Niebuhr:

> *God grant me the serenity*
> *to accept the things I cannot change;*
> *courage to change the things I can;*
> *and wisdom to know the difference.*

My focus was on the things I could change. So, I created two checklists. First, I created a checklist containing things that I had no control over, such as the residual effects of having undergone four neck surgeries and the pathologies associated with these conditions. I couldn't change these any more than I could change the weather.

My second checklist contained the things I could do something about. These were areas in my life where I could affect change. No matter how slight the changes were, if they were attainable, I wrote them down on my second checklist. This section included crystal clear changes I needed to make, such as losing weight, improving my metabolism through diet and exercise, as well as changing my attitude about life.

This approach may make everything seem clear and simple. But the fact was I felt totally overwhelmed by all that I had to do. When I looked at my two lists, it seemed that there were many more uncontrollable factors than there were improvements I could actually do something about.

For instance, I felt compelled to lose weight in my pursuit of transformation. But, I wasn't hoping to shed a mere 10 or 20 pounds. I needed to lose at least 50 pounds to regain any sense of respectability, and to reach that target weight, I knew I had to exercise. And I had let pain prohibit me from doing that for a number of years. In fact, whenever I lifted anything over five pounds, this action caused excruciating pain in my neck, and sent burning nerve pulses down both legs. This was just one example of the many sympathetic nervous system problems I was forced to confront on my journey of transformation.

There were times when it seemed that I could control nothing on either one of my lists. My mind was willing to embrace a new life, but my body stubbornly resisted. My body used the battle scars from past surgeries and the blubber shaking from my mid-section to raise doubts about my journey, and suggested that I was too far gone to make any measurable changes.

At times, it seemed that doubt attempted to seize my soul, invade my deepest thoughts and dampen all my hopes for a better life. During those times when doubt was winning the battle, I would become overwhelmed at the prospect of dealing with all the issues I needed to address.

At times it seemed that my desire for change and the forces of the past were engaged in a spiritual battle between my spirit and my body. It appeared that my tired body was going to win the victory, but my spirit raised its powerful voice from the bottom of my soul, providing fresh visions of healthiness along with calm and encouraging thoughts about the road ahead.

When I settled my mind enough to assess my situation, I realized I didn't need to do anything spectacular or superhuman to counteract my many imperfections. I simply needed to affirm the one thing that would keep me on the journey of transformation: my commitment to change.

Starting a journey toward a new life isn't good enough. If we set out on a new course of change, what's essential is staying the course, regardless of how many obstacles and distractions try to misdirect our well-intentioned steps toward change.

Over time, the longer we act upon what we believe, the stronger our beliefs will become. The growing strength of our beliefs help us do what we need to do to remain obedient to our vision and continue the journey.

This process resembles the things a person goes through while climbing Pikes Peak, or one of Colorado's many other 14,000-foot-high mountains. At first, the mountain seems too big to conquer. But as we go higher, step by step, the mountain seems more manageable. Following through on our commitment to reach the summit challenges everything we say we believe and forces us to use every resource at our disposal in the ascent: mind, body and heart.

The further we go in the journey of transformation, the less fear we have. If our core values and deepest beliefs are a solid part of our foundation, they will not give way when they are tested by doubts or fears or trials. In fact, the more our beliefs are tested, the stronger and more confident we become in them.

This kind of strength comes from the inside and enables us to handle nearly every form of calamity that life doles out. This strength empowers us to confront our fears, pains, losses, and disappointments from the past. It helps us walk through the fire and emerge whole on the other side.

Doubt tried assailing me on many fronts, including a direct assault on my beliefs, my core values, and my hope for a better future. But instead of avoiding my problems or procrastinating about what to do next, I remained resilient and continued the journey of transformation. In the end, only by staying on course could my life be changed.

Fully Believing

Doubt had also tried to assail my belief in God. Like many people, some of my experiences with religion had left me dumbfounded about what to believe, especially when pain and loss screamed much louder than God's assurances.

Some people believe they can change their lives on their own, but I knew I needed God to help me be transformed. So when doubts made me question whether I was really seeing proof of his power and grace in my life, these doubts also jeopardized my healing and growth.

There's no such thing as partially believing in God's grace, especially when it comes to sustaining the journey to a better life.

In a sense, God provides a safety net for each one of us as we climb our own mountains of pain and regret. There are times when I look down from a particularly dangerous part of the climb and I try to see with my own physical vision. In those moments I experience fear as I see myself dangling on a rope thousands of feet above the ground. I cringe to think about the outcome should I slip and fall.

But, when I look at things from the perspective of belief in God's loving grace, the climb doesn't scare me so much, because I know he will catch me, restore me, and set me on my feet again.

If I were to attempt transformation on my own, without any belief in God, my dreams of newness and healthier living would have crashed to the ground as a plane unable to break gravity's power on takeoff.

Belief emboldens us, helping us to think, and act differently than we have done in the past. Trust in God provides us with spiritual eyes that enhance our ability to see things from an eternal perspective and then to act accordingly.

Even if we're dangling on a rope that's hanging from a cliff that seems miles above deadly hazards far below, we do not have to be consumed with fear. Instead, as God works within our own spirits we can see a new vision of how things can turn out. With God's help, we will reach a safe, sheltered ledge, providing a foundation for our present and our future.

There's a passage in John's Gospel that explores how belief can help us experience God's eternal power. Here's the setting. Jesus has been crucified. He had risen from the dead and appeared to his confused disciples. He not only commended his disciples for their faith, but also sent a message to people like you and me who would come to believe in him during the centuries to come:

Have you believed because you have seen me? Blessed are those who have not seen and yet have believed (John 20: 29).

Weak Belief in a Strong God

It's not the strength of your belief that matters. It's actually the strength of the thing in which you believe. Having a strong faith in a weak chair won't prevent you from landing on the floor. But even a weak faith in a strong chair will allow you to sit quite comfortably.

Thankfully, God really exists. And while he doesn't need me to believe in him, I need him to believe in me.   B u t there's a second important aspect of belief, and it's something many of us tend to forget.

God promises that he will reward those who diligently seek him (Hebrews 11:6b). That means you and I are not alone in our pursuit of transformed living. God is with us as we try to scale the impossible parts of our mountain climb.

We're not really transforming ourselves through self-belief, even though we've seen some marvelous demonstrations of the human spirit. We do our part in the journey as we walk step by step, but ultimately God is the One who makes the changes within us as we place our lives into his hands.

If you've ever hiked in the mountains, you've probably seen how green forests give way to rocky slopes incapable of sustaining visible life. But, if you walk or hike here in the Rocky Mountains, you can often witness the impossible: such as a sturdy tree growing from a cliff's sheer rock face.

Not only is this sight mind-boggling, but it is also beautiful. It's a symbol of how the impossible can happen through God's intervention, his participation in our lives.

Although we can't always identify precisely how this spiritual growth is occurring in our lives, we can tell something is at work that transcends our own abilities to change our lives. But the purpose is not to "explain" God or put him in our box; the purpose is to surrender ourselves to him in order to grow beyond our own inadequacies.

Wouldn't you like to see the entirety of your life flourish as splendidly as the mountain tree that flourishes despite its impossible odds and rocky circumstances? For those who believe in God, the impossible is possible!

Though you might not be able to see what's next for yourself with your own eyes, I encourage you to believe in him first. He'll reward you by taking off the blinders of a hardened heart so that you can see far beyond what you see in the world today.

God will also provide you with an eternal optimism that fortifies your hope and gives you the strength to climb a little higher each day. As you continue on your journey, step by step, and day by day, you will encounter unimaginable new discoveries. You will experience the kinds of beauty and splendor that can only be experienced on your journey of transformation.

I encourage you to keep climbing! And when you feel like looking down, look to God instead!

Insights for the Journey

- Doubt tries to convince you that you can't fulfill your dreams. It wants you to remain stuck in your past life. To break free from your past you need to combat doubt by holding tight to your core beliefs while you experience new things and incorporate newer, healthier habits into your lifestyle.

- In your walk of transformation, the first day out of the gates is application day. It's the day when you act on your sense of urgency to journey toward change, no matter what. Practical change begins when you put it into motion and believe it will happen for you.

- Change takes place in the here-and-now. Your activity and present-day lifestyle will determine the course of your future.

- Don't take on more than you can bite off and chew in the process of transformation. Instead, work on one thing at a time to remain on your course of change.

- God will help you on the journey of transformation if you believe in him. Believing begins with trusting in the existence of God. It continues with God rewarding those who believe in him. When you start to *fully* believe in him, then you've truly entered into a radical lifestyle of faith.

PART TWO

Five

• • • • •

Rebuilding a Broken Life

People regularly rebuild their communities following destruction caused by storms, volcanoes or war. Debris is cleared away, new structures rise from the ashes, schools and hospitals are rebuilt, and trade is revived.

The Bible story of Nehemiah describes a rebuilding effort focused on the wall surrounding the city of Jerusalem. The wall, which had been broken down during the Babylonian siege, no longer offered protection to the city's residents. Someone needed to lead the rebuilding effort. Nehemiah was the right man for the job.

Today, you can buy hundreds of books about Nehemiah, many of them focusing on his leadership and management abilities. That's because Nehemiah did what was required in order to get the job done.

But what happens when we are rebuilding a life instead of a wall? What if we are hoping to transform our bodies, minds, emotions and wills into something stronger, more resilient and more life-giving to others?

The first half of this book explored what it means to start the reconstruction process with the help of solitude, pain, and an awareness of what needs to be done. In this second half of the book, I am going to look at the tools—including attitudes and actions—we will need to complete the process of rebuilding our lives.

Tools for a Successful Remodeling Project

I don't know if you've ever had the pleasure of remodeling your home. Perhaps, using the word "pleasure" is a bit of a jab to those who have endured this onerous process. I've heard contractors compare the remodeling process to giving birth. There is great delight and celebration once your new kitchen or bathroom is finally ready, yet the process often involves many unexpected twists and painful trials.

Each building project carries its own unique set of quirks. There are between 60,000 and 90,000 parts and pieces in a newly constructed home. If your builder gets 99% of your project completed perfectly, then this means that you might find 600 to 900 flaws in your new dream home. If your builder of choice constructs your home to a 99.99% level of perfection, then 6 to 9 building imperfections will still be found. Imagine how quickly the number of imperfections would escalate if you were trying to rebuild a human body, with its 100 trillion cells, 640 muscles, 206 bones, 22 internal organs, 100,000 hairs and 60,000 miles of arteries, veins and capillaries.

The possibilities for a major mishap are enormous. But we can learn from Nehemiah as we seek to rebuild our lives.

For one thing, we will need a sense of mission. If we don't think the project is worth the effort, we will lose heart and may never complete it.

We also need to do our homework. Nehemiah conducted careful research about the task at hand. He quietly walked around the city by night, without fanfare or unwanted input, surveying the extent of the problem and perhaps formulating some tentative strategies for his massive project.

The ability to adapt to adversity is also important. Many people run from adversity, but those who succeed anticipate how they will deal with it. Those who succeed never give in or run from the fight.

In the first half of this book, I also wrote about the importance of inviting God to be a part of the process of transformation. This one Psalm in particular illustrates how important God can be to the rebuilding process:

Unless the Lord builds the house, those who build it labor in vain. Unless the Lord watches over the city, the watchman stays awake in vain (Psalm 127:1).

In the case of Nehemiah, he was smart enough to realize that he couldn't rebuild Jerusalem's walls on his own. He needed God's help, and that help actually made it possible for the walls to be rebuilt, and within a relatively short time.

In my case, I knew I couldn't effectively manage to rebuild my own life alone. I knew I needed a worthy Master Craftsman who had the wisdom to help me to come up with the kind of power that would help me accomplish the task that lay ahead. I needed to lose weight and then, to keep those pounds from returning again, recreate a higher purpose for my life.

I needed Jesus, who is the architect of our faith, to provide an exact blueprint for me to follow. I needed his understanding of my dreams, and I hoped he would make these align with what it means to live the transformed lifestyle. I needed him to coordinate all the pieces of my body, soul and spirit together to make me whole again. I needed his grace to cover over my weaknesses, and for his Spirit to give me the strength to endure the jolting episodes of reconstruction that might cause disillusionment or doubt.

These were the tools I needed to begin my rebuilding project. Then, it was time to get to work. Here are some of the steps that helped me along the way.

Inspect for Damage

Experienced contractors will warn you that their cost estimates for your new kitchen or bath may change if they encounter unexpected problems. The best way to avoid nasty surprises is to survey the damage carefully. That means before you start to stack the cement blocks, one on top of another, hold off for a time, stand back, and draw a plan of what you're trying to recreate.

I had to first believe in the vision of God's finished work that he had shown me. Then, I had to inspect and assess the damage to my broken body before I started to rebuild my life and make the changes that were needed. Was it possible for my body to be rebuilt along slimmer lines? That would require significant work to my current, out-of-shape figure. I needed to see things the way God saw them and allow him to guide me toward the best methods to accomplish my desires for a new, more active and healthier lifestyle.

I once asked a contractor to bid on a house project. But, after I told him about all the project's complications, he told me the job was more than he could handle. He wanted to tackle a smaller project.

God knows exactly what shape we're in. He knows if our foundations are weak or if our walls are buckling. And thankfully, he takes on difficult projects because he loves redeeming seemingly impossible people situations!

Still, it's important for us to be honest with ourselves and God by conducting a full assessment of the true damage we have done to our lives. Doing this is our way of handing over the entirety of our life and our needs to him.

Give God the full details about your true condition, including both your physical blemishes and your deeper problems beneath the surface. Let him know that you can't make all the required repairs by yourself. Acknowledge that you need expert assistance to guide you through the process. Then begin to surrender to him your desire to do the work accordingly.

Let God know about your vulnerability, your fragility and your fear. The truth is, you're not sure you will survive another failed reconstruction project. Even if you could endure another quick fix attempt, you fear you are placing your own future in jeopardy. Thoughts that another bad self-improvement project may cause irreparable damage might persist.

I craved to lose at least 50 pounds and was fully inspired to do so, but I feared I would repeat the mistakes I had made in the past. I didn't want to revert back to my old ways of relying on my own sense of self-sufficiency and self-preservation.

I desired that God would be the foreman of my rebuilding project, simultaneously remaking my mind, body and soul. I also wanted to be willing to learn from anybody that the foreman wanted to employ for the project, whether that be people I would encounter while transitioning to work, at church, or at home.

What I really wanted was to let God rebuild my ransacked soul and create a house of hope. That would require that I maintain a clean slate with God. My inspection report needed to reflect my commitment to this new reconstruction project in the right way.

Instead of Frank Sinatra, who sang about how he did it "My Way," I was tired of my way. I wanted to do things God's way. I wanted to trust in him more fully than I ever had before. I wanted to experience his loving power on a deeper, more intimate level.

Perhaps you have seen a painting or poster showing Jesus knocking on a door. The image conveys that Jesus wants to enter the house of your life if you will open the door, but he won't barge in uninvited.

Jesus is probably knocking at your door right now. He does that to all of us all of the time. How will you respond when you hear the knock at your door? I hope you will let him in. He's a much needed guest.

Don't be too hard on yourself during the reconstruction process. You may get tired of the noise and the sawdust and the chaos, but think of how nice things will be when the project is completed.

There might be some pain involved as old roots are removed to make way for a new foundation, but that pain will be temporary. The new life that is being built in you can last forever.

Building a Bodily Temple

I wish God had given me a detailed set of blueprints for me to follow, but that's not what happened. That's not how faith works. Instead of receiving instructions telling me how to move from Point A to Point B in my journey of reconstruction, my spiritual life seemed silent and barren. I knew I had a long way to go in changing my life, but I lacked direction and felt like a forlorn tumbleweed being blown this way and that, across hot desert sands.

It's a common dilemma. Some people who realize they need divine help say they want God to take complete control of their lives. But God doesn't work that way—at least not in my experience. Although he's in the business of changing peoples' lives, he doesn't exert himself upon us in a way that violates our free will.

We are called to be God's servants, not his robots. Even though he *could* wave a magic wand and miraculously heal every physical and emotional wound, he typically takes a subtler role, providing us with strength and courage but leaving most of the heavy lifting to us.

This is generally true, but in some cases, God clearly gets more involved. The Bible records many of these cases, including the creation of two magnificent structures where people could gather to worship. God provided precise architectural plans for the construction of Solomon's Temple (found in the Old Testament books of Samuel and Kings) and Zerubbabal's Temple, also known as the Second Temple (found in the books of Ezra and Chronicles).

In the cases of these two temples, God developed the detailed plans and humans provided the labor and materials as a sign of their devotion and dedication.

In my case, I didn't have an operating manual from on high. But what I did have was a transforming vision, faith, and this powerful passage from the Apostle Paul:

> *Do you not know that your body is a temple of the Holy Spirit within you, whom you have from God* (1 Corinthians 6:19a).

Ideally, the condition of our bodies should reflect the purity of our souls. But that wasn't the way things were in my life. In my heart, I desired to be healthy and happy, but for years my body had been at war with my soul. Instead of my body reflecting the inward beauty of a temple where God is worshipped and obeyed, it was sadly doing the opposite, as evidenced by my outward state of dilapidation.

Yes, it would have been nice to see God ride in on a white horse and clean me up from top to bottom, but I was beginning to see that God wanted to be my partner in the reconstruction of my life, not the sole laborer.

My part of the project was becoming clearer. I had to gather information as honestly as I could about my worn-out condition. That meant I had to take precise measurements of my entire body, inside and out. And, like the workmen constructing the holy temples of God, I needed to roll up my sleeves and get to work, showing my own devotion and dedication.

Building a Foundation of Facts

Every building requires a solid foundation, or the structure will be unstable and unsound. In my case, the foundation would begin to be built with facts. I wanted to know everything I could about the reality of my situation before I devised and implemented a plan for improving things.

The first thing I did was to consult my physician about my health. Though I had lived with chronic pain for several years, and there was no evidence that this might ameliorate any time soon; it was imperative that I establish a solid baseline about my condition. Thankfully, my physical exam showed that I didn't have any evidence of clinical instability following my many neck surgeries.

I also requested a complete blood count, hoping that the information would equip me to combat my obesity problem. My doctor also ordered a chemical study of my lipid profile. The results were shocking to me, both as the caretaker of my body and as a former healthcare practitioner.

My triglycerides, cholesterol and LDL levels had sky-rocketed way beyond acceptable ranges. Consequently, my doctor gave me a prescription to help reduce my very high cholesterol levels, and another medication was prescribed to assist in jump-starting my body's inactive metabolic system.

I also purchased a scale and began weighing myself twice a day, first in the morning and then before going to bed in the evening. I started 225 pounds. I had a 42" waist, an 18.5" neck, and I wore an XL-XXL shirt size. These figures may not be too bad for a professional football player or a Sumo wrestler, but connecting these numbers to my 5'7" frame revealed my body's pitiful state. Though I once had a sharp clinical understanding about preventive health measures, it seemed as if I had lost all my knowledge by the way I had been living since my injuries.

The more facts I compiled, the more dire my scenario seemed. Clearly, my outer temple did not reflect the inner awareness I possessed about living in a healthy, balanced way. With God engaging with me to triumph over my weakened life, I knew I needed to move from research to reconstruction. It was time to start putting my new plans into action.

First Things First

Many journeys fail before they begin because people have unrealistic expectations. But, as Nehemiah's wall wasn't built in a day, my journey of reconstruction would also be a long-term project.

Therefore, I did not construct an overly elaborate plan for my journey. I didn't weigh myself down with impossible goals to accomplish. Instead I kept the process very simple. My goal was to make and maintain the commitment to diligently seek God in the small, practical steps of walking off the extra pounds I had carried for the last decade.

First, I needed my body and its life-giving systems, which were dormant, to awaken, and to react to some healthier ways of living. Did you know that low fitness is a reliable predictor of early death? That's right—it's even more effective than gauging other factors, such as smoking, consuming alcohol, being overweight and having high blood pressure and cholesterol levels.

It's not surprising that walking for 30 minutes per day actually has a tremendous impact on our health, in terms of preventive measures. So, walking became a big part of my plans to reengineer my very, out-of-shape body. Most experts say physical exercise is essential to healthy living. Given my history of inactivity, obesity and chronic neuropathic pain, walking was an obvious way to get started.

I also started making some radical dietary changes. Out with the old processed foods and in with the organic fruits and vegetables. I drank plenty of alkaline water and eliminated any caffeinated or soft drinks. I also found diet plans and menus in magazines and online that I taped to the refrigerator to remind me that my new eating program could be both healthy and tasty.

I kept adding plans to my bodily reconstruction. I concentrated on incorporating new ways to change some of my behaviors, such as using smaller plates, practicing proper food-combining techniques, scheduling four meals per day, as well as not eating after 5:00 p.m. most evenings.

To keep myself focused on making the changes that needed to happen, I wrote things out for myself to review often, much like an architect or engineer would develop blueprints for himself to reference regularly. This gave me more time to study and reflect on these ideas before acting on them with all my heart.

I also tried to avoid unrealistic timelines. I estimated that my journey of reconstruction might take as long as the birthing process, approximately nine months. It was really a process of new birth for my life. Accordingly, I planned to lose about 1.5 pounds per week during the next nine months of my life. I knew this was only a start, and there would be a second phase to the rebuilding process. In fact, while I believe, in a sense, that we're constantly under reconstruction, I needed a more finite timeline for the most dramatic changes, so I started focusing on losing the extra weight in a way that seemed entirely doable.

If you had been watching me from the balcony, you might have concluded that I had become extreme in my zeal. I purchased new workout clothes, new running shoes, a new treadmill, and other tools and trappings I believed would help strengthen my motivation to succeed. Not everyone will want to spend money on equipment like I did, but I knew that would help me follow through on my commitment to change.

Clothes don't necessarily make the man, and exercise clothes don't inevitably lead to a slimmer waistline, but I was embracing a radical new lifestyle, and I felt I needed to get rid of the old to bring in the new.

I also needed all the encouragement I could get, even if it came from myself. That's why I went downstairs and wrote some encouraging messages near the new treadmill. I used a blue Sharpie marker to write the following messages on the wall in our unfinished basement:

"Don't stop."

"Get skinny."

"Keep in the center."

"Stay on the path."

In the coming months I would need to spend countless hours on this treadmill. At times, when my dedication was tempted to wane, these short, simple and inspiring messages would help me stay the course and remain committed to the journey, step by painful step.

From Passions to Plans

Each one of us dreams of living a better life, but how many of us transform those dreams into an action plan that will yield the desired results?

My plans, which were simple and clear, helped me rebuild my life by replacing my old behaviors with new habits. By being committed to this reconstruction project, I became excited to worship God with a physical temple that was daily becoming more and more like the temple God wanted for me and for himself.

There were times on the treadmill when I felt all alone. But, most of the time, I knew God was with me, helping me grow my vision for a better life - giving me more power than I possessed on my own, and gradually revealing more of his wonderful plans for my future.

What about you? Are you ready to create some concrete plans for your rebuilding campaign? Are you willing to do the required research? Can you write down your plans, and then follow them up with commitments of time and energy and attention so they can become your pathway to deeper transformation?

The road ahead may look daunting, but come along with me. If I can do it, you can too. There will be no looking back. You'll have to leave behind much of your heavy baggage from your past. Just keep your eyes on the road ahead and ask God to help you do the best you can as you take those individual, small steps toward a transformed you!

Insights for Rebuilding Your Life

- Your life is a constant reconstruction project. There are too many unexpected trials to throw you off course. You must have a specific plan to keep the project moving forward and help avoid the unnecessary pitfalls.

- Inspect your damaged life and give a full report to God. Don't leave anything out. Consider this a wonderful opportunity. It's the disclosure process of change. From the broken parts, your new life is going to be rebuilt.

- Acquire measurements of your entire body, inside and out, to start the process of change and to gauge the progress of your reconstruction.

- Write down your plans, then follow through with them. Resolve to maintain your commitment to changing your life. Keep the process as simple as possible when beginning the preliminary action steps.

Six

• • • • • •

Obeying Your New Vision

It's the year 2043, and the apocalypse has come and gone, turning America into a dark, barren, ash-covered landscape. But not all is dead. A man named Eli sets off across the country on a mission to serve and protect a book of sacred scriptures that holds the solutions to humanity's problems.

If you saw the 2010 movie, "The Book of Eli," starring Denzel Washington, you know that Eli's goal throughout the movie is to "stay on the path" that he had been called to take.

Eli's journey seems difficult, if not impossible, but he gets help from unknown, unexpected sources that protect him and his sacred book from the violent gang members who survive in this devastated world by preying on others. That protection succeeds so well that people who encounter Eli are amazed. Some even ask if he is more than just a man, or if he has angels or other supernatural powers keeping him safe.

I don't want to ruin the movie for you by giving away any of its secrets and plot twists. But "The Book of Eli" remains one of my favorites. Even though it is dark and disturbing at times, it is ultimately a hopeful portrayal of a man who obeys a calling that he may not fully understand. Eli was instructed to go West. Eli didn't know what this mission would entail, but that was OK. He obeyed the vision, no matter what, with no questions asked.

I sometimes think about "The Book of Eli" as I travel on my own journey of healing and transformation. I have been trying to "stay on the path" ever since God confronted me during my bathroom mirror epiphany, showing me how far I had fallen and pointing me toward a better life.

Like Eli, I am also protecting a book—the book that you are reading right now. My book may not hold the solutions to humanity's problems, but I believe it could be helpful to many who want to start walking on the path toward a better tomorrow.

People seek transformation in different ways. Some take a cafeteria approach, sampling various systems of diet, exercise and therapy until they find a mix of methods that work for them. For me, the cafeteria approach doesn't work. I get so distracted by all the competing options that I lose my focus and waste energy. That's why I believe in single-minded obedience to an inspired vision.

For me, success requires being obedient to a specific vision. I know that some people don't like the concept of obedience, which they associate with compliance, conformity and subordination. They prefer to go their own way. Understandable, but you can benefit from the immense power that comes from being solidly committed to worthwhile objectives of change.

What about you? Do you have trouble staying on the path? Are you tired of going down dead-end roads that don't really get you any closer to your destination? Are you frustrated after trying everything and finding that nothing really works?

Let's take a look at this under-appreciated concept of obedience, which is something that can help keep us on our journey to "stay on the path" toward transformation.

Getting There Starts with the First Steps

Thousands of years before a fictional Eli roamed a barren, post-apocalyptic landscape, there was a brave fighter named Samson. This brave and bold Old Testament figure once wrestled a lion with his bare hands and annihilated an army of 1,000 Philistines with only the jawbone of an ass for a weapon.

But, things got tough for Samson. Betrayed by the seduction of Delilah, he allowed his hair to be shaved from his head, thus breaking his Nazirite vow to God. With this disobedience he lost his supernatural strength. Ultimately, he also lost his sight. His eyes were gouged out by Philistine soldiers' swords and Samson was taken as prisoner to Gaza, where he worked a woman's job of grinding grain to make bread.

I've never wrestled lions nor single-handedly taken down an entire army, but I do feel a kinship with Samson because I know what it feels like to lose my strength, both personally and professionally. Perhaps you have as well. You could also say that I lost the eyesight of my heart and became imprisoned by my own pain and miseries. I was seduced, too. It was not a woman who tempted me; instead, I suffered the consequences of spiritual adultery whenever I disobeyed God's will and tried to make my dreams come true in my own way.

One very clear example of my spiritual adultery happened during the years that I tried to replace God's vision of my life with a self-absorbed take on the American Dream. These were the years when I simultaneously attempted to serve God and money. Even though Jesus had clearly warned against attempting this, I thought "having it all" was my pathway to the abundant life.

Of course, I wasn't the only person trying to serve both God and mammon (Matthew 6:24). It is a common practice in churches across America. But, being common doesn't make something right. Instead of being content with what I already had, I lusted after more and pushed myself harder to pursue the things many of us desire: esteem, financial security and a taste of the "good things" in life.

Plain and simple, this approach never really panned out for me, relative to it lasting over the entire course of my life. My American dream led to a nightmare, and like Samson, I found myself stripped of what I did have. Instead of starting my journey by taking those first steps in the right direction, I pursued dead ends and rabbit trails that took me farther away from God's goal for my life.

Samson's punishment for disobeying his vows involved hard labor, day after day, on an ancient stone treadmill, where he slowly and methodically turned the big, stone wheels that ground grain into flour. Much of my punishment took place on a modern, high-tech treadmill, where I slowly and methodically tried to turn my big, bloated body into something healthier and happier.

I took one step after another, step by step. Through sheer determination and the fear of failure, I was able to keep motivated during the initial few weeks of my new regimen on the treadmill. Each day I did the same routine: I walked; then I walked some more; then I kept on walking. Pretty soon, I was on a roll. I started walking faster and for longer distances.

I kept telling myself to keep going. I kept looking at the wall in front of me as I walked on the treadmill, trying to obey those encouraging messages that I myself had written on our unfinished basement drywall, which I had mentioned in the last chapter:

"Don't stop."

"Get skinny."

"Keep in the center."

"Stay on the path."

I knew I needed to obey these messages or it would be too easy for me to give in and give up. I had to keep walking, taking step after step in blind obedience, no matter how tired I felt or how pointless things might have seemed. My companions were the hum of the treadmill motor and the "fwop, fwop" sound of my mid-section flab bouncing back and forth with each step I took.

At first, I felt absolutely ridiculous. I could remember a time when I was physically on top of my game, maintaining a vigorous schedule of exercise and fitness. That was then. Now was a different matter. I found it difficult to continue walking on the treadmill, even though it was at the lowest possible speed (a measly one mile per hour) for the shortest period (10 whole minutes!), on the lowest possible incline (zero).

As I walked step after step, I asked myself: Will this tiny and seemingly insignificant effort ever produce any tangible results? It didn't seem so at the time. Instead, I felt awkward and fragile as I embarked upon what seemed to be an impossible journey of change.

If you've ever attempted *anything* significant, you've been there. The first steps are so important, but they can be so frustrating. We all need to begin somewhere, but unfortunately for most of us, we have to start from a place where we never wanted to be in the first place.

That's life. It's not like the checkout line at the store or the passing lane on the highway, where you can try to cut ahead of somebody else. There are no exemptions from the work required to stage a comeback in life. And, it does absolutely no good to dwell on our sorrows about past failures.

"Don't stop," said the writing on the wall, and I knew I had to obey. I had to stay on the path. I needed to turn my eye away from anything that would seduce me away from the vision that God had given me. Even when these bright and inspiring images were beginning to fade to black during the earliest phases of my workouts, I knew I had to obey these promptings from God.

Did it seem like I had experienced the vision ages ago? Yes, but I had to keep walking. Did I feel foolish at times for sticking with my program? Of course, but I had to stay on track. Would I feel relief if I just quit my workout and relaxed with a diet soda or a pint of Italian ice cream? Of course, temporarily, but I had to obey God's vision for my whole life by doing what he called me to do now. To stop meant choosing a path of destruction.

It was like I was in a voting booth and none of the candidates knocked me out. I could not just vote for anybody, as that would be a waste. So, instead, I voted for the least-worst candidate. My options were not great, but I know the choice to continue through my first painful steps on the treadmill would pay off in the end. The other options were not so promising.

Life's a Marathon, Not a Sprint

Marathon races were an important part of the ancient Greek Olympic Games; and they remain popular around the world today.

Modern, officially sanctioned marathon races began again in 1896. American runner Johnny Hayes ran the 42-kilometer course in just over two hours and fifty-five minutes. Just over one hundred years later, Kenyan runner, Patrick Makau, ran the 2011 Berlin marathon in a time of 2:03:38. In a century, athletes have trimmed nearly an hour off the time required to run 26.2 miles.

I admire those men and women who push themselves to break records that earlier generations of athletes considered unbreakable. Such victories speak volumes about the power of the human spirit to accomplish great things.

But, I am not a marathon runner. In an effort to overcome my own life obstacles, I tried to muscle my way through each day in order to become part of the life-changing process. My efforts revealed tremendous courage I wasn't sure I had. Nonetheless, we all have some measure of courage deep down. But the truth is that most people will eventually become burned-out as their adrenaline levels fizzle during the process of trying to make strides toward remarkable change. At least that's what almost happened to me.

And that's precisely where obedience saved me. Realizing that I couldn't triumph over all the obstacles in my path, I put my trust in God instead of myself. I rested in his vision for me instead of trying to become an overnight sensation. Instead of trying to conquer all my enemies, I learned to surrender to God for strength and guidance on my marathon of transformation, one step at a time.

As the starting gun fired and the race began, I sprang from the blocks full of energy and positive emotions, feeling that I was ready to do whatever it took to win, or at least finish the race. I felt the rush of spiritual endorphins coursing through me and lifting me up when I felt low. For an instant I felt I was already well on my way to a new life that would usher me into the land of milk and honey.

But neither my strongest emotions nor my best intentions were enough to secure my victory. In fact, I practically tripped over my own shoelaces in a desperate lunge just out of the starting blocks.

You see, I had not trained for a marathon, and I didn't yet have the endurance for a long-range race. In fact, I had many broken parts that needed attention. Instead of racing to the finish line, I actually needed to go back and learn how to crawl.

So, that's what I did, starting with a baby's crawl before relearning to walk. In time I was moving at a brisk pace, and before long, I had reached the midway point of the race, feeling stronger and healthier with every step.

That didn't mean there weren't setbacks and painful recuperations. I experienced what anyone does when working with less-than-perfect bodies or strained circumstances. I faced additional breakdowns along the course. The bottom of my right foot developed a painful neuroma. Different areas of my body experienced new levels of pain and muscle cramping. Meanwhile, the healthy alterations I was making in my diet didn't seem to provide enough nourishment to maintain the stamina that I needed. To top it off, at times, the brightness of my optimism began to flicker and fade during the harder parts of the race.

Sound familiar? You have probably experienced similar challenges as you have run your own race. No matter what race you are running, there are many unexpected surprises along the way. And at times it seems as if powerful opposing forces want to spoil your plans by devising new crises when you are just struggling to stay on the path.

When you feel like you are being ambushed, or that enemies are throwing banana peels in your path, or that pain is halting you dead in your tracks, this is not time to stop. Perhaps, it's time to slow down a bit and realize that the goal is reaching the finish line, not killing yourself by trying to break the speed records.

If you've survived the first steps of your journey but are beginning to face challenges in the middle of the course, you are free to adjust your pace. Instead of loading your shoulders with performance pressure, take a deep breath and dial it back a notch. Change some of your workout times or routines. Reshuffle the types of food that you eat. Try to accomplish projects in shorter bursts of time. Schedule your day so you do the things that need to get done when you have the time and energy to do them, rather than stretching the day out, but with less effectiveness.

But, whatever you do, do not stop!

It's OK for you to be the tortoise, and not the hare, so long as you keep your eye on the finish line and remain obedient to the transforming vision that will see you through to the end.

Food for the Soul

Samson realized that life was a marathon, not a sprint. Even though he had fallen far from his original strength and status, he didn't accept this low point as a "new normal." Even though he suffered horribly in the Gaza prison, he labored endlessly to transform his life and make it better.

As we saw, Samson was sentenced to slave at work on the large stone treadmill that turned grain into flour. In time, the hard work helped him regain his strength. Eventually, his hair grew long again. Soon, Samson even regained his confidence in God.

Samson's story ends in a shocking event that would make a great scene in a 3D movie. The blind Samson is removed from prison and brought out to perform for the crowds attending one of the Philistines' pagan religious festivals; an event dedicated to the god Dagon.

"Our god has delivered our enemy into our hands,"
shouted the crowd, "the one who laid waste our
land and multiplied our slain" (Judges 16:24).

But Samson saw an opportunity for getting revenge on his captors. He asked a servant to guide him to the pillars of Dagon's temple. Once there, he grabbed the pillars and—crying out to God for strength—knocked the pillars down, killing the Philistine rulers, and himself in the process.

You may not like the ending of the story, but it illustrates an important point: that a strong and successful person can lose it all—strength, esteem and success—and then regain much of what was lost.

Samson's renewal happened on two levels: the physical and the spiritual. On the physical level, Samson worked hard at the task he was assigned on the treadmill, slowly but surely rebuilding his bodily strength. This is similar to what you and I can do on the physical level: exercising; eating better; losing weight; changing our diets; improving our negative attitudes; controlling spending; and breaking away from our addictions.

But, bodily work alone is not enough to bring true transformation. Like Samson, we need to attend to our souls through prayer, repentance for our sins, and submission to God's will for our lives. This sounds easy, but it's not. Just as physical change takes time and energy, the journey of transformation requires our full commitment and patience.

Spiritual transformation also requires our full attention, just like a marathon race. You may have seen runners or other athletes drinking energy beverages as they compete so they can replenish lost nutrients. The best energy drink for the spiritual journey is the Bible, which is more than a mere collection of words in a book. The Word of God is alive, and can bring life to us.

After God called Ezekiel to be a prophet, God gave him a strange command: "Eat this book." Here's how Ezekiel explained the command, and his response:

> *And he said to me, "Son of man, feed your belly with this scroll I give you and fill your stomach with it." Then I ate it, and it was in my mouth as sweet as honey* (Ezekiel 3:3).

Imagine. What would it be like to try to eat the parched paper sewn between leathery bindings? Ezekiel didn't care. He reverently did what God commanded of him. To his delight, he ate the scroll and it tasted as sweet as honey.

He tasted the fruit of contentment that was produced from obedience.

Likewise, God wants you and me to study his living Word and ingest it into our innermost being. Consuming the Word helps us to maintain moral purity, which keeps us on the right track as we journey toward transformation. Studying the Bible inspires us to follow the ways of God. The Word helps raise us to higher standards of living, rather than allowing us to settle for lower cravings and leftover crumbs.

Like Ezekiel, I ate the Word of God. I didn't actually eat the pages out of the Bible, but I certainly began reading it more closely. I went deeper into passages I had never heard or even read before to find hidden treasures that would bring strength to my life. I also mediated on the Word in bite-sized morsels, savoring their flavors and insights, by taking a verse or two and dwelling on them all day.

My newfound devotion to the Word of God provided me with much needed sustenance and brought peace to my soul. The more I ate, the more I developed a palate for studying and meditating on the Word. In time, I was changing from the inside out. Reading and studying was no longer an onerous chore. It became a way of life, just as sitting down to the table to eat my next meal. And the more I ingested the Word, the more I wanted to know who God really is and what he really desires from me.

Obedience Feeds Bodies and Souls

Jesus once said, "I am the bread of life; whoever comes to me shall not hunger, and whoever believes in me shall never thirst" (John 6:35). It was a remarkable claim, but my own experience has proven it to be true, as so many others have experienced as well.

Transformation requires both spiritual and physical obedience. In addition to my soul eating God's Word, I have also been more discerning about what my body consumes.

Often, spiritual and physical nourishment work together to sustain and strengthen us. During the day, I typically ate four small meals so I could acquire the right amount of fruits, vegetables and proteins required to properly nourish my body. I rarely ate any food after 5:00 pm. in the evening.

This regimen meant that I still felt ravenously hungry at times, especially later in the evenings. But rather than eating additional meals or snacking into the later hours to satisfy these cravings, I chose to hand over my feelings of hunger to God through sacrificial prayer, followed by a brief study in the Word. I chose to train my body through spiritual practices, instead of obeying the hunger pangs from my body.

If you've ever heard doctors or nutritionists talk about healthy eating, they will usually promote a "balanced" approach that involves eating various foods to achieve the right balance. In my journey, I have learned that a balanced approach to life transformation requires proper amounts of both physical and spiritual sustenance. Think of it as sprouts *and* spirit.

Are you willing to be obedient to the requirements of complete life transformation, both bodily and spiritually? Are you willing to create a balanced diet for both your body and your soul? If so, you will be able to experience the journey of transformation more fully.

Insights for the Journey

- "Stay on the path" of transformation. You might slip, but you will never completely fall if you have a spiritual companion to pick you up. God will strengthen and protect you along the way.
- Face the fact that you cannot avoid the physical and spiritual preparation required to make a comeback in life. Ignore the short cuts and focus instead on achieving the long-term dreams you have for your life.
- Don't rely solely on your own strength or stamina to survive the grueling process of change. Learn what it means to obey God with your life. This will help you to counteract any emerging feelings of becoming burned-out.
- Feed your soul with the bread of life. You can practically do this by studying and praying

over the Word of God. If you need a fresh start, then consider daily reading the Word for 20 minutes, then praying for 10 minutes what you had just read deep into your heart.

Seven

● ● ● ● ● ● ●

Self-Discipline for Body, Mind and Spirit

Shortly after my bathroom epiphany, history was made September 1, 2006, even though you didn't read about it in the news or study it in a history class. That's because this major event happened in my basement, and I was the only person who witnessed it.

After years of trying to rise above some of the limitations associated with my pain, I finally did it. I got on my treadmill, turned it on, and started walking, step after step after step.

This may not seem like a big deal to you, but it was a history-changing event for me. Even better, I repeated the workout the next morning, and the next. The result is that ever since that day in the fall of 2006 I have worked out on my treadmill at least six days per week, walking the equivalent of 15 to 18 miles every week.

This means that over the past five years, with God's grace, I have walked over 4,300 miles. I checked my atlas, and the distance from Maine to California is nearly three thousand miles. I am now eagerly looking forward to the day when I will complete my second transcontinental treadmill trek.

I don't need to tell you how many times in the past I intended to start exercising. You have probably faced similar struggles yourself, whether it's keeping your New Year's resolutions or simply following through on other promises and pledges you have made to improve your life.

Unfortunately, promises and pledges don't always translate into action, nor do great ideas always result in successfully completed projects. It's like H. Jackson Brown, Jr., author of the bestselling *Life's Little Instruction Book*, put it, "Talent without discipline is like an octopus on roller skates. There's plenty of movement, but you never know if it's going to be forward, backwards, or sideways."

Or, think about how the ancient Greek philosopher Plato explained it: "The first and best victory is to conquer self."

No matter who the messenger is, the message is the same: there's one essential ingredient you will need in order to succeed on your journey of transformation. You need self-discipline.

Our word "discipline" comes from the word for "disciple," who is someone that follows a particular teacher and/or code of life. Plato had disciples. Jesus had disciples. In both cases, the disciple based his or her life around the master's teaching.

Those individuals who could not follow through were not considered good disciples, even if they said "I agree!" or shouted "Amen!" to everything the master taught.

Self-discipline describes the ability to motivate yourself to do things no matter how you feel about it and regardless of the challenges you face. Does self-discipline require you to immediately walk 4,300 miles? Of course, not. You have your own unique challenges and callings. But you will need willpower, persistence and self-discipline to take your first step, and then the second, and the third.

I estimate that I have taken nearly nine million steps on my treadmill. But if I had known on Sept. 1, 2006 that so many steps stretched ahead of me, I might never have taken that first step.

That's why I needed self-discipline to rein in my fears and anxieties. You need self-discipline, too, if you want to successfully complete your own journey.

Unpopular but Powerful

If you asked people in a research survey what their favorite topics were, I don't think discipline would make the Top 10. That's because most of us have mixed emotions about discipline, which is often related to other least-favorite topics like failure and punishment.

In the past, I had a mixed track record with self-discipline. I was always able to motivate myself to work hard on a business initiative or an intellectual problem, methodically plugging away until I had achieved my goal.

My problems arose when my willpower ran smack into the wall of my physical pain. To begin a workout regimen meant that I would not only need to combat my inertia but I would also need to face my powerful archenemy: pain.

Each one of my steps on the treadmill sent "Ouch!" messages ricocheting through my central nervous system. Self-discipline helped me to keep these pain messages in perspective so I didn't over-dramatize them or allow them to paralyze me. In time, my steps felt easier and more natural, even though they never became pain-free.

What about you? What are the challenges that stare you down and strike fear into your heart as you seek your own transformation?

Each one of us faces a difficult world. Life isn't full of sunshine every day. Quite frankly, it's brutal out there. We're bombarded by all kinds of stresses. Meanwhile, your body issues its own demands, enticing you with physical impulses that seem to demand immediate satisfaction.

To be disciplined means fighting against these trials and temptations with an iron will, resisting any self-indulgence that comes your way. It means to remain single-focused on the immediate task ahead.

What's your own personal history with self-discipline? If yours has been a rocky road, why not take a fresh look at discipline and do whatever you can to make it your friend.

A Three-Part Challenge

What was the biggest challenge when I started my new treadmill routine?

Was it a *mental* challenge, based on my previous negative history with trying to cope with seemingly unsolvable problems?

Was it a *physical* challenge that primarily tested my body, my physical inertia and my pain issues?

Or was it a *spiritual* challenge related to determining what kind of response I would make to the vision I had been given for a transformed life?

Here's my answer to these questions: YES! Self-discipline challenged my mind, body and spirit.

This is an issue of anthropology as much as theology. The question is: how do you view human beings? Are we rational creatures? Do we even have the ability to change our lives?

In my view, we are created in three aspects: body, mind and spirit. Therefore, transformation needs to take place on all three levels if it is going to be meaningful and lasting.

That's why the remainder of this chapter will show you how self-discipline is a journey of going both inward and outward. You need to go inward to address the mental habits or emotional issues or spiritual hang-ups that will weaken your resolve. You also need to go outward to ensure that your commitment to transformation is being realized in your body and your behavior.

True transformation can't be "virtual." It needs to be "actual," and that involves reflection, beliefs and actions.

Putting Self-Discipline into Practice

Your body, mind and spirit need to be on the same page as you seek self-discipline in your life. Let me show you how this worked for me as I sought to make my dreams and visions for a better me become a reality in my life.

1) Dietary Discipline

It is estimated that roughly one-third of Americans are overweight or obese. Not long ago, I was among the obese, too, weighing sixty pounds more than I should have. Thankfully, I have developed the discipline to tame my appetites and eating habits, which limits my food intake.

If I could discipline this part of my life, I believe you can, too. The techniques that worked for me may not be the best techniques for you, but you can use my approaches until ideas of your own present themselves. I mentioned some of these in an earlier chapter, but I feel like I need to elaborate further in order to aptly encourage the practice of self-discipline.

Over the years, the size of the average American plate has grown ever larger. I'm not talking about servings (though, those have grown too), but the actual plates we use to serve and eat our food. I decided to do something about that, and it was actually one part of my dietary discipline that was relatively easy: I ate my meals from salad-sized plates instead of the larger-sized dinner plates that had been the norm for so many years.

Before, I used to try to pile as much food as possible on the biggest plates I could find. Even then, I wasn't always satisfied, thinking about dessert as I quickly stuffed my mouth. Now, I get a medium-sized plate and arrange the food so the various servings fit neatly on the plate and look nice.

This plate technique worked pretty well, so I decided to try the same thing with my utensils. One method that worked for me was to eat my meals with a salad fork instead of the larger, longer-tined forks I had used before. This may seem like I am trying to play mental tricks on myself, and in a way, that's true. On the most basic level, I was trying to redefine normal. As part of this program, it was essential that I change the way my brain processed reality. The old normal was killing me, so I was ready for new ways. Using smaller utensils helped me retrain my brain about what constituted a "normal" serving or bite of food.

But I didn't rely only on plates and forks. I also became more intentional about eating the proper amounts of food instead of gorging myself until I was full. At first I used measuring cups to measure out perfect four- or five-ounce portions of proteins, vegetables and grains. In time, I could measure my portions by comparing them to the size of the palm of my hand.

In addition to changing how I ate, I also rearranged when I ate. Instead of eating three large meals a day, I had four smaller meals per day, finishing my last meal by 5:00 p.m. so I wouldn't fill myself before bedtime and not have a chance to burn those calories off.

In the bad old days, there was a kind of ravenous hunger to the way I ate, trying to fill what seemed like an endless cavity. Now, as I eat, I try to pace myself, savoring each bite instead of rapidly moving on to the next. I may not be a card-carrying member of the international "Slow Food" movement, but I sympathize with their efforts to transform mealtime from an eat/more/faster approach to a quieter, slower experience that finds fulfillment in quality, not quantity.

One of the best things I did was to wage all-out war on empty calories by resisting the intense urge to eat decadent desserts loaded with their sugars and fats. For too long I had allowed myself to eat harmful desserts as a reward of some kind, but the reward I was seeking now was a new me. Desserts were one of my biggest enemies so I was relentless in my fight. I am thankful to report that during the first 13 months of my new dietary regimen, I didn't eat one dessert!

When we had dark chocolates or Italian ice cream in the refrigerator, I'd look at them, determined not to indulge in these delights. It was tough at first, but I soon found that the more I resisted, the more strength I developed to follow my vision. The resistance was a valuable form of self-discipline.

Instead of eating sweets, I popped chewable Vitamin C's tablets. This not only curbed my sweet tooth but also gave my body increased antioxidant support.

I also got intentional about the things I drank throughout the day. The Institute of Medicine says that men need about three liters of liquid a day (that's about 13 cups), and women need about 2.2 liters (around 9 cups). Some people find it easier to follow the 8-8 approach (eight glasses of eight ounces each).

Either way, we need liquid, but many of us do what I did: slaking our thirst with caffeinated and sugared drinks, like coffee and soda drinks, that don't really help us at all. I decided to drink only the best beverage all the time: water. And that included alkaline water as well.

But, I was addicted to sugar and caffeine; a fact that was proven to me once I made the change to water. I went through the typical, but difficult, withdrawal symptoms. I experienced pounding headaches, dehydration, ringing in the ears, mood irritability and fatigue for three or four weeks. You would have thought I was trying to kick cocaine or heroin. This uncomfortable period wasn't much fun, but I knew I needed to cleanse my system, break my addictions, and stop polluting myself.

What about you? Do you struggle with what you eat? You've seen the way I wrestled with my own culinary habits. What do you think would work best for you? Take a minute or two and write down some concrete ideas that sound appealing to you.

Some people think about diets as a matter of the body, but my experience shows that effective self-discipline involves body, mind and spirit working together to create a better life.

There were times when it seemed like my mind was playing a leading role in the battle, as when I had to persuade myself to stick with my new water regimen even though my body was rebelling against the idea.

At other times, my body was helping the process by adapting to a new normal and being satisfied with less instead of more.

My spirit was also a key player as I sought to cooperate with God's Spirit in finding a new way to live. At times when my body and mind were weak and powerless, my spirit reminded me of the vision of the transformed life I was pursuing. In order to obey that vision, I now needed the discipline to put it into practice.

I believe the same three-way approach of mind, body and spirit will serve you too.

Let's take the approaches I used in disciplining what I put into my body and see how we can apply them to the issue of exercise.

2) Disciplining the Body

People become overweight and out of shape for a variety of reasons, so you need to employ a variety of techniques to confront these bodily challenges. The body is the focus of the battle, but mental and spiritual weapons are equally important.

I've already told you about my ongoing transcontinental treadmill journey. But let me take you behind the scenes of this private, history-making event. As I explained in the last chapter, exercise of any kind was very difficult, at first. When I started out, I walked so slowly that I wasn't getting any "distance." Instead of despairing and giving up, I sometimes worked out a few times per day.

After the first month, I was walking briskly for at least 35 minutes per day. All I could think of was to be obedient to God's vision for me to become thinner and healthier. To be obedient, I knew I had to be self-disciplined so I could see the fullness of my vision become reality. My mind was hard as flint. I refused to think about stopping, no matter how I felt. And believe me, I felt terrible most days, having many episodes of pain.

Scheduling my workouts was also a challenge, so I typically worked out early each morning, before my wife (or even the roosters) was awake. This decision was mental, physical and spiritual. My mind drove the process, while my body reluctantly came along for the ride.

What was most amazing was the way my spirit benefitted from the workouts. When I went to bed at night, I would actually look forward to my morning workout time with God. If you've ever been to a gym, you can see people watching TV or listening to an iPod. But I wanted to listen for God's voice during the pre-dawn hikes in my basement. At times I worshipped God. Other times I thanked him for inspiring me to begin making urgent changes.

At times I could feel my body, mind and spirit moving together as one. I knew God's ways were the right ways, so I just kept walking by faith. But, the walk was also a physical walk, and the more focused I became, the more determined I was to finish each workout to the best of my ability.

I never looked too far into the future regarding my workouts. I remained in the present, making sure to move briskly so I could walk between 2.5 miles and 3.1 miles, which took me 35 minutes, and 42 minutes, respectively.

I could precisely predict when the sweat droplets would start pouring from my head, at about the 15-minute mark of my walk. The more drenched I became the more invigorated I felt, because I knew I was disciplining my body in new and significant ways.

The walking also helped reduce the stress that was caused by my daily, unceasing and chronic pain. By disciplining my mind, I could channel my thinking away from the pain and toward the destination I was trying to reach on my journey.

My journey was lightened by an "attitude of gratitude." This may sound like a cliché, but just because something is a cliché doesn't mean it isn't true!

Most mornings, I was awakened either by my pain or by my inner alarm clock, usually before 5:30 a.m. As you may know, this is a great time of day to gripe and moan and complain about how bad you feel and how little sleep you got. I tried to make these early wake-ups a great time for thanking God for my life and for the chance to make a new start. I would climb out of bed—trying not to wake Cherise (my beautiful and faithful wife of 16 years)—and thank God for giving me the chance to wake up to a blessed day. What a gift each new day is when you receive it as a gift and thank the giver.

Being thankful deepened my capacity for self-discipline in so many ways. When I sensed I was tempted to quit my workouts, I would recite out loud all the things I was thankful for. When I started these recitations it was difficult, but in time I realized how many great and wonderful gifts I had received. When I pondered these gifts and thanked God for them, I found my attitude of gratitude growing. I even thanked God for allowing me to work out every morning.

I also had another companion with me on the treadmill: Rocky Balboa. I was a big fan of the Rocky movies, and I shared the popular Sylvester Stallone character's simple approach to personal transformation. My experience wasn't like one of the glitzy TV shows where someone's life and house are remodeled in 60 minutes. Like Rocky, my journey of redemption was solitary and far from glamorous. I, too, was getting back to my roots and reacquainting myself with the good old American work ethic.

While Rocky was training for the big fight, my workouts were not a competitive thing. For me, my morning sessions were times of surrendering to a higher purpose, training myself in mental toughness, and curbing emotions that remained stubborn against the spiritual side of life.

Of course, the biggest helper was the Holy Spirit, whom Jesus referred to as our "Helper." There were times I sensed God's Spirit within me, giving me the strength I needed to remain self-disciplined. But, even when I didn't feel God's presence, I kept on walking.

As for my pain, it never totally disappeared. Instead, it waxed and waned, coming on strong at some times and temporarily subsiding at other times. Eventually, the pain exerted less control over my life, though realistic limitations still existed, such as having a five-pound lifting restriction and the onset of rheumatoid arthritis, for instance.

Step by step, I walked on, believing that my time of faithfulness in the small things of life would help me develop self-discipline in bigger things. Continued self-discipline was my demonstration of walking out my faith and placing complete trust in God to help me rebuild my broken life.

3) Spiritual Disciplines

When I wasn't on the treadmill, there was another discipline I utilized to help me strengthen my spirit. It was simple and practical but yielded otherworldly benefits.

Every day I would read the Bible for 20 minutes before meditating and praying on what I had read for another 10 minutes. This simple exercise impacted not only my mind (every day I was filling my mind with biblical teaching and concepts) but also my heart. As I meditated on these truths, they became more real and more alive.

Surveys show that 89 percent of Americans have a Bible in their homes, but having it doesn't necessarily equal reading it. Only 59 percent of Americans say they read the Bible occasionally, with only 21 percent saying they read it weekly and 16 percent saying they read it every day.

What about you? Do you believe that spiritual growth is more than merely a *mental* activity? Do you believe that God wants to touch your spirit as well as your mind? Have you ever devoted quality time to reading and reflecting on the Word of God?

The more I did this the more I felt I was changing mentally, spiritually, and even physically. Whenever we study the Word of God, we can literally step into another dimension of time and taste eternity. This action toward God pulls us away from remaining completely attached to the world, and opens our eyes to a broader vision of what God is doing in the world. For someone who could often focus too narrowly on my own issues and problems, having a broader view helped me to become more centered in God's will.

I didn't create this discipline of Bible reading combined with meditation and prayer. Christian monks have been practicing "lectio divina," meaning a "divine reading" of the scriptures for more than 1,500 years. It's one of the spiritual disciplines that have become a regular part of life not only for monks and nuns, but also for millions of normal men and women who want their relationship with God to grow deeper and impact more areas of their lives.

Many Forms of Discipline

If I had a few hundred more pages in this book I would love to describe the other spiritual disciplines that can change your life and your faith:

- Fasting
- Solitude and silence
- Simplicity and frugality
- Service and giving

Since I don't have a few hundred more pages, I will simply recommend Richard Foster's best-selling 1978 book, *Celebration of Discipline*, which helped re-introduce many Protestants to these powerful but often forgotten practices.

Insights for the Journey

- If you want to walk across the country (or across the room), discipline yourself so you don't worry about the enormity of the task before you, but instead, envision the destination and the progress this will signify for you and your journey of transformation.

- Seek to have your mind, body and spirit work together as one so your self-discipline in one area will help you in all areas.

- If you need to change your diet, change as much as you can about your eating habits, including what you eat, how much you eat, when you eat and how often you eat.

- When it comes to physical exercise, start with something simple that works for you and once you are successful with this activity, add another form of exercise to your physical regimen.

- Feed your spirit with the Word of God. But don't just read the words and let them slip from your mind. Rather, read deeply, then meditate and pray on the passages you have read so they can enter your heart and transform your life.

Eight

• • • • • • • •

The Healing Power
of Connection

If you've ever been to Hawaii you've probably heard of Father Damien, the Catholic priest who volunteered to work with leprosy patients that had been isolated on a remote peninsula of land called Molokai.

After leprosy and other diseases imported by traders and sailors to the Hawaiian islands caused a health crisis of suffering and death for the local population, the Hawaiian legislature passed the "Act to Prevent the Spread of Leprosy" in 1865. The act served to isolate hundreds of people with leprosy (also known as Hansen's disease), who were rounded up and quarantined away from all social contact with the outside world.

The local Catholic bishop felt he couldn't force one of his priests to work at the leper colony. It turns out he didn't need to, because Father Damien, a young priest from Belgium, volunteered to serve the lepers. Father Damien threw himself into the work of caring for 816 quarantined lepers, addressing their wounds, and helping them build homes where they could live.

There's one other important thing Father Damien did with the lepers. He loved them. He reached out to them. He graced them with the gift of human contact that they had been longing for since they had been gathered up and separated from their families and loved ones.

Have you ever felt that other people have treated you like a leper? Maybe they were congenial friends or co-workers until you started having problems. Then, once they realized you were suffering, they withdrew their love and support.

We live at a time when technology allows Americans to connect electronically with people on the other side of the world. Many of us connect to others by using our ever-present smart phones to send messages or Tweets to Facebook friends or Twitter followers. But technology can never replace face-to-face interaction and the kinds of heart-to-heart sharing that happen when two people meet for coffee or a meal.

The challenge of connecting can become even more difficult for people who suffer from deep physical, emotional or spiritual pain. For many of these people, the experience of isolation only adds to their feelings of rejection, discomfort and loss.

I believe each and every one of us is designed for connection. Our connected lives begin when we're born into families, and the connections continue where we grow up in neighborhoods, or become involved with communities of peers at work, at church, or in our social activities.

But oftentimes, people in pain feel about as welcome in these social circles as Hawaii's lepers felt on their isolated peninsula. That's too bad, because people in pain need connection with others as well. Plus, people in pain have a lot of insight they can share with others. Let me explain as I describe a few ways connection can be a powerful healing force.

Wired for Community

None of us were born into a "perfect" family, but even imperfect families practice connection. If you've had a rough day at school or work, you can come home to your family expecting to experience a basic level of love and acceptance.

And if you can't find the connecting support within the home, other institutions and groups also try to mirror aspects of these family bonds. For example, street gangs have a strong allure for young men from troubled families, as the relationships within the gang help make up for the absence of solid familial bonds.

Even after we grow up and leave our families of birth, we don't live alone. Our joys and happiness are better when we have others who are willing to share our pain and burdens.

The Christian vision of the spiritual family is spelled out eloquently in Paul's passage about the body:

> *For just as the body is one and has many members, and all the members of the body, though many, are one body, so it is with Christ. For in one Spirit we were all baptized into one body – Jews or Greeks, whether slaves or free – and all were made to drink of one Spirit.*
>
> *For the body does not consist of one member but many. If the foot should say, "Because I am not a hand, I do not belong to the body," that would not make it any less a part of the body. And if the ear should say, "Because I am not an eye, I do not belong to the body," that would not make it less a part of the body. If the whole body were an eye, where would be the sense of hearing? If the whole body were an ear, where would be the sense of smell? But as it is, God arranged the members in the body, each of them, as he chose. If all were a single member, where would the body be? As it is, there are many members, yet one body.*
>
> *The eye cannot say to the hand, "I have no need of you," nor again the head to the feet, "I have*

no need of you." On the contrary, the parts of the body that seem to be weaker are indispensable, and on those parts of the body that we think less honorable we bestow more abundant honor, and our unpresentable parts are treated with greater modesty, which our more presentable parts do not require. But God has so composed the body, giving greater honor to the part that lacked it, that there may be no division in the body, but that the members may have the same care for one another. If one member suffers, all suffer together; if one member is honored, all rejoice together (1 Corinthians 12: 12-26).

I love this description of how the various parts of the church can work together to create one body. The foot, the hand, the ear—and even the aching neck—depend on each other, with each part contributing to the whole and with each part's strengths compensating for the weaknesses of the other parts.

This passage also teaches a radical equality that is at the heart of the Gospel. As Paul sees it, both the leper and the priest are treated with equal honor. That's where the power of connection is undeniable. Interconnecting the stronger to the weaker serves to strengthen all the members in the body. There are times when we need our injuries attended to, or to be pampered by having our feet washed, or also to be given a cup of cool water during our desert excursions.

Paul's words reveal the transforming power of connection. No matter who we are or what we're going through, community is better than solitude. Two—or three, or a hundred—is better than one.

The fact is, all of us have learned things in our journey through life that can help others on their journeys. This kind of wisdom is not something that should be hoarded, but rather shared with others in the context of community. Instead, we should be willing to step out of our personal comfort zones by stepping into the reality of other people's lives so we can share the lessons we have learned while receiving the wisdom and comfort of others.

That's why Jesus said the two greatest commandments were to love God and love your neighbor (Matthew 22:37-40). The two are linked, and the people who say they love God but never connect in a deep way with the men and women in their lives are missing something essential.

Most of us hunger for community, but that doesn't mean we're very good at building it. Particularly when we're experiencing physical, emotional or spiritual pain, our temptation is to turn inward and disconnect from others. But these tough times are when we need community most. The community needs us, too, for it is in the healing connection between various members of the body that the life-transforming power of God is made manifest.

When Community Fails

Many of us have witnessed the power of community that Paul describes. The young willingly care for those who are older. Those with resources care for those who are experiencing the burdens of misfortunes. The healthy provide comfort to the suffering. Everyone lends a helping hand to care for the orphans and widows.

Unfortunately, some of us have also seen communities that fail to act as the spiritual body in Paul's description. I know that when surgeries and pain and obesity became bigger factors in my life, many of my brothers and sisters in the faith withdrew from me.

Initially, I thought that perhaps they didn't really realize I was in pain or that I needed their support. The fact was, they *did* realize I was in pain, and once they realized it they quickly did everything they could to get as far away from me as they possibly could. Sadly, this was true of both lay people and their leaders. Where was my Father Damien when I needed him to reach me with his healing touch?

"Why are my friends abandoning me?" I asked. In time, I came to understand that people basically view suffering as a form of leprosy. Of course, they're sad for those who suffer. But they want to keep their distance so that the suffering of others won't infect them and lessen their own chances for happiness.

Paul taught that the various parts of the body should serve one another, but the members of *my* Christian body seemed to fear my pain and suffering as something that might be contagious. Instead of welcoming pain in their midst as a path to deeper intimacy with God and with others, they kept me at a safe distance, much as an NFL running back uses a stiff arm to keep tacklers at bay.

Rather than serving as healing communities like Father Damien's leper colony, some churches have become insensitive to those in their midst who weep, choosing to sweep pain and suffering under the carpet. As a result, some churches are neglecting to care for the broken parts of the body.

Churches aren't the only groups that are experiencing a decline in social capital. As Robert Putnam pointed out in his bestselling 2000 book, *Bowling Alone*, the last quarter century has witnessed a 58% drop in people who attend club meetings, a 43% drop in the number of families that share dinners, and a 35% drop in having friends over.

What is it that is causing our communities to weaken and fail when people need them most? And where can people who suffer turn for the love and support and connection they need?

Helping the Blind to See

It is said that anyone who has lost his eyesight can make better use of the other senses, such as hearing or touch, to compensate for the blindness. The same can be said for those who have experienced significant physical pain and suffering. People who suffer bodily pain and emotional anguish often devote greater energy to spiritual growth and development.

On the other hand, when life is going great, God is often ignored or relegated to a position of lesser importance. After all, when our bank accounts are full, our health is good, our children are excelling, and everything in life is coming up roses, we don't feel a need for God because we believe we're successfully in control of life.

Have you seen this in your own life? When we experience pain, hardship and loss that are too much for us to handle, we turn back to God, seeking his power and grace to make our lives better again. Often we do so in the hope that something miraculous will relieve us of our pain and our burdens.

Like a blind man, I have learned that regardless of whether I am experiencing good times or bad times, I have looked to see beyond my pain and loss so that I can focus on God and surrender my life to him. This has allowed me to see the spiritual aspects of life more clearly, just as the blind man might learn to hear sounds more acutely.

The same thing can happen for you. If you're living with chronic pain, you can pay more attention to the spiritual dimensions of life. This can help you develop a deeper understanding of suffering that leads to spiritual purification and transformation. Your losses can be transformed into gifts that can bless not only your life but can also be shared with members of your family and community.

Those who struggle with pain naturally desire to be pain free. But for some of us, freedom from pain isn't in the cards. I wish God would explain to us the mysteries of pain and suffering. But in the meantime, he comforts us and gives us the grace to continue the journey of life.

The comfort we experience is not ours alone but is designed to be shared with others in the body, as Paul explains:

> *God of all comfort, who comforts us in all our affliction so that we will be able to comfort those who are in any affliction, with the comfort with which we ourselves are comforted by God* (2 Corinthians 1:4).

The weak can be made strong by the hand of God. They can receive an intimate injection of his grace. As a result, these seemingly weak links in the church community have powerful gifts of comfort that can be shared with others.

No community is perfect, since each group is made up of broken and fallen human beings like you and me. So, if you feel your community has rejected or failed you, don't retreat into your own private cell. Instead, be willing to roll up your sleeves and seek new ways to become involved in the lives of others. This kind of loving service will not only help you on your journey of transformation, but will also help others on their journeys, as well.

Finding Community Close At Hand

Each one of us responds differently when it seems that a community chooses to treat us like lepers rather than love us with open arms. In my case, I quit trying to "fit in" at church. I still attended weekly services, but I increasingly felt like a stranger who didn't belong in a community that did not understand the complexities of suffering or know how to provide comfort to those who suffered.

I determined that if the hands and feet of the church body didn't want to support my aching neck, I would invest my energy in initiatives and ministries that fed the hungry, cared for orphans, evangelized those who were unchurched, or focused on ministering to youth or missionaries.

Yes, I was involved with the body of Christ. But, I still felt alone and displaced until I discovered a community that was close at hand in my wife Cherise, who has become the closest human connection in my life.

When Cherise and I were married in 1996, neither one of us knew the kinds of pain and struggle that I would be enduring through the course of our marriage. But shortly after we said, "I do," I was increasingly forced to say, "I can't" to many aspects of my normal life because of the pain I was suffering.

Every marriage is a journey, but ours has had more than its fair share of twists and turns. Let me turn things over to Cherise, so she can tell you herself how she felt and how she responded.

An Unexpected Love Story

I had just moved from Texas to Colorado, taking with me my four-year-old son as we sought to start a fresh life in the Wild West.

I was seeking my Romeo and I found him in Gordon, who instead of focusing on the mistakes of my past viewed me as a woman who was pure and sanctified by the power of God's incredible grace.

Gordon instantly connected with me on many levels and helped me experience a depth that I had not experienced in any previous relationship with a man. My son also connected with Gordon's seven-year-old son. We were married 21 days after we met and I was amazed to see my new husband serve as a strong spiritual leader, an incredible dad and a loving husband.

Every love story has its challenges, and ours was no exception. We had no idea that Gordon would endure increased levels of pain, but six months into our marriage, Gordon developed Complex Regional Pain Syndrome (CRPS). His doctors told me to be prepared because he was going to die.

I was shocked. I had dreamed of a bright future together including more children, more "honeymoon experiences," and for Gordon to be able to work. Now, all of this seemed out of the question.

Gordon had a serious talk with me, encouraging me to get my real estate license so that I would be able to stand on my own two feet if something grave were to happen to him. I threw myself into my new real estate career while also taking care of the boys and caring for Gordon's needs in those critical months of acute agony.

At the church we were attending, I gathered the courage to ask my women's group to pray for Gordon. They obliged but then quickly turned the conversation back to an upcoming women's cookie bake sale. At that moment my cookies certainly became baked alright! My disconnection from the church began in my heart that day as I concluded Gordon and I must make our journey alone.

I had other doubts, too. Would I run or stay with my beloved? It was tempting to leave. I was a woman with a huge sense of adventure. There were mountains to climb, slopes to ski, oceans to dive, jet skis to race, and the list goes on.

I confess that at times I resembled Job's first wife. When Job experienced extreme suffering, his wife encouraged him by suggesting he curse God and die. That's dark, I know. But it was so hard to tolerate Gordon's agony and not be able to help him.

I stayed, but the realities of Gordon's physical suffering impacted every area of our lives. There was the role reversal that had made me the sole breadwinner. There was also the realization that I would not be able to enjoy "normal" activities with my husband. From that day forward I struggled to fight back against feelings of self-pity and disappointment. There was so much that I had hoped for in our marriage, and instead got the opposite.

Even during Gordon's darkest moments, he said, "We are still going to praise God." Together, we thanked God for our lives and his blessings. And as we invited God into the depths of our disappointment, his grace overcame our despair. In time I began to see that losing my plan "A" paved the way for God's plan "B," which offered greater blessings than I ever could have imagined.

Gordon once told me he wouldn't have asked me to marry him if he had known about the pain and problems we would be forced to endure, but I'm glad we married when we did so he wouldn't endure this life alone.

People who suffer chronic physical or emotional pain often doubt that they are worthy of love, yet Gordon was worthy (and so are you). Marriage has changed us both in powerful ways. The joy we have experienced has transcended Gordon's physical limitations. He is still the man I fell in love with 16 years ago, and he retains every attribute that first drew me to him.

Gordon demonstrates what it means to live a transformed life in the midst of pain. He has been the backbone of our family, showing up every day at school to get the boys and giving 100% to being a loving husband and father. And on those days when I fall into the depths of depression, he gently leads me back to a place of hope. He brings life, humor, discipline, and deep faith into our daily routine.

In a sense, Gordon is a silent hero. Every day he overcomes his pain, finding hidden treasures to share with me and with others who need his help.

Through God's grace and Gordon's coaching from the sidelines, I have been able to build a thriving real estate business. This role reversal was not something I had ever desired, but it has helped transform my own selfishness and sense of entitlement. Work has been healing for me and allowed me a space where I could contribute and feel productive.

Our family has also grown. Our boys have now grown into young men who possess great sensitivity, strength and empathy for others.

The life that Gordon and I share is not easy, but I look at him today with a sense of love that is hard to express. It is like two people who have been in a foxhole together in the middle of exploding bombs; fighting for each other. Our love has grown through adversity. Gordon is known as a motivator not only to me but also to others who depend on his wisdom and insight for their own trials.

Today, more than anything, our unique love story continues to grow.

Caring Enough to Connect

Pain has a way of separating us from those we love and need. But even if others treat you like a leper, don't let their behavior define you. Instead of finding a cave and crawling deep inside, open yourself up to the love of God and others. If you do, you will soon see how this love you share can transform you from the inside out.

Insights for the Journey

- You do not have to remain quarantined from others just because you might be experiencing horrendous pain, brokenness and loss. Regardless of what part you represent in your community or the body of Christ, you belong to a bigger vision.

- Two are always better than one. Let God's love tear down any walls you might have built up against another person. Your story is not yours to keep secret. Experience the

---

transforming power of God by sharing your life in community with others.

- Being in community with others can be very messy. There are always political and personal differences that try to divide any group, even in the church today. Practice the power of forgiveness to overcome any discrimination or brewing conflict among your community.

- People with chronic pain who have focused on the spiritual side of life may have a great depth of insight to share with others. The comfort they have received from God can help them provide comfort and encouragement to others if they are allowed to share these gifts.

- Remain committed to your relationships, even if the road seems like it is taking you in the wrong direction. Love conquers all and can help you finish your life story in a beautiful way.

Nine

• • • • • • • • •

Emerging from the Darkness

The lights in the room were bright, even brilliant. But, as I lay on the operating table that August morning, all I could feel was darkness. That's because I didn't want to be in this hospital room for another, in my seemingly never-ending, series of neck operations.

"Why?" I asked no one in particular. "Why this? Why me? Why again?"

Without realizing it, or willing it, I slipped farther into a dark hole of doubt, despair and troubling questions.

Will I ever open my eyes again, or will this surgery be the last of me?

If I survive, how much will my body hurt during recovery?

Will the surgery help me, or will I feel even worse afterwards?

And how many disks can be taken out of my neck before it rebels and pleads, "No more!"?

As my body lay there in that bright room surrounded by nurses, my heart was falling deeper and deeper into a dark place of pain, fear and dread.

I had already seen this movie many times before. The ending was supposed to be a happy one, featuring a smiling patient who was cured of his chronic pain. But the pain never left, and the surgeries just kept on coming. No wonder my heart felt despondent.

Have you ever felt this way about recurring problems and setbacks in your life? I have. I described this feeling in the first words of this book: I vividly remember the day my neurosurgeon labeled me as *totally and permanently disabled.*"

It may seem like we have come full circle only to arrive back at the same place we started. But my journey hasn't been a circular one. Instead, my journey has taken me to a better place. No, I'm not free of pain and problems. But now, when I find myself entering into a dark place, there's a difference in how I respond.

In the old days, the fear and dread would get the best of me - but not anymore. Although I don't seek out the dark and painful places of life, I now accept them as part of the picture.

Instead of complaining and protesting, I now accept the darkness and seek to learn and grow from it. Instead of yelling at God as the darkness envelops me, I reach out to him and embrace him in the midst of the darkness, asking him to guide me and love me.

Suffering has a way of taking us to the darkest places of our hearts. But, ironically, it's those dark places that teach us and change us. If we are willing to grow from our encounters with the darkness, they can become a launching pad for our journey of transformation.

Unfairly Imprisoned

Thankfully I've never been incarcerated for a crime, but I've known the feeling of being trapped in a cage, unable to enjoy freedom or safety. This experience helps me identify with a biblical character that is known for his triumph over suffering. Not Job, as you might expect, and who has his own book of the Bible, but Joseph, whose story is told in the latter portions of the book of Genesis.

Much of Joseph's life was filled with overwhelming atrocities and unfair punishment. But, despite the cruel treatment he endured, Joseph remained faithful to God. That's why he is my poster boy for transforming darkness into light.

You probably know portions of Joseph's story. Born to Jacob and Rachel, Joseph was loved more than his brothers. His father even gave him a coat of many colors to show his favored position. The jealousy grew so strong that his brothers even plotted to kill him before deciding to let him live.

Joseph was thrown into an empty waterhole and later sold into slavery.

What do you do when you are the victim of an injustice? I know what I am inclined to do, even if it's temporary. I kick, scream and complain about my fate. Not Joseph, who was purchased to serve Potiphar, a rich man and the captain of Pharaoh's guard. Instead of letting the darkness get the upper hand, Joseph focused on the light, doing such a good job with his work that he was promoted as a superintendent over Potiphar's entire household. That's a decent job for a slave!

Soon, Potiphar's wife tried to seduce Joseph. When she was unsuccessful, she channeled her feelings of rejection into a plan of revenge, accusing him of seducing her. As a result of her fabricated claim, Joseph was unjustly thrown into prison.

Once again, Joseph had an opportunity to rant and rave and condemn God for his fate. Instead, he dedicated himself even more fully to God, who helped Joseph's dark prison become a school for transformation.

My story isn't as dramatic as Joseph's, but I've experienced a similar kind of up-and-down trajectory, feeling hopeful one moment and then becoming ensnared again in the despair and darkness of life.

My darkness was not an actual prison; it was a prison of suffering caused by my obesity and chronic pain. I hoped to transcend the troubles of my past and change into a healthier and happier person who could walk up a flight of stairs without passing out, enjoy life with my wife and coworkers, and be an example of the good things God does for his children.

My journey of transformation is by no means over, but it is well underway, and I have much to be thankful for. Instead of toting around a 42" waist and an XL-XXL shirt size, I trimmed down my body to a 31-32" waist and a small shirt size. Similar changes were under way internally. My blood work changed dramatically, and my doctor told me that I had normal ranges in each of my blood panels. He even compared me to a healthy individual half my age.

I was doing it. I had conquered my weight, my fears, and my limitations. I was excited about taking the next steps in my walk of faith.

Things were going great in these areas for several years, then, out of the blue, something unexpected happened. I developed a new pain-producing condition: an aggressive attack of rheumatoid arthritis that caused acute joint pain and nodular swelling in my feet, ankles, knees, hips, wrists and fingers.

The physical pain and emotional anguish had me reeling, reopening my old emotional wounds and sending me again into a place of darkness and despair. Like Joseph, I had made great strides in confronting my circumstances only to wind up imprisoned once again. I felt like I was back at the beginning again, revisiting a place that through God's grace and my own hard work I had left long ago.

Light in a Cave

How you look at things greatly impacts what you see. If you mention the word "cave" to my mother, she will immediately think of bats and cringe. But, if you mention caves to amateur cavers and spelunkers, you'll generate as much excitement as some of us feel about a vacation in Australia or a trip to Disney World.

These varied reactions reflect humanity's long history with caves, which have been used for many purposes, including protection from enemies, shelter from inclement weather, or long-term residences for some of our ancient ancestors. Some unique caves even house beautiful works of art. In France's Lascaux cave or the Altamira caves in Spain, ancient artists created drawings and paintings on cave walls that still inspire awe today.

One thing you can count on in most caves is darkness, but there are different ways to look at darkness. In my experience, it isn't all bad. Sure, if I had my choice I would rather live completely in the light. But that doesn't mean darkness should always cause anxiety or resistance within our souls.

The journey of transformation takes place in both light and darkness. As we walk, the path is not always illuminated with bright light. And when we find ourselves walking in darkness, we need to rely on the mercies of God to navigate through the hidden tunnels, slippery passageways and tight spots in our hearts. When our hearts return to the darkness, we have an opportunity to develop our eyes of faith. Total darkness moves our eyes off the things we continually see in the world and inspires them toward an attitude of dependence upon God.

When my return trip to the operating table for another neck surgery led me to a place of darkness, I instinctively recoiled in fear. But it doesn't need to be that way. We may not want to embrace the darkness, but at least we can take a fresh look at the painful wounds of our past and discern if these former battle scars can harm us any longer on our quest for abundant living.

Exploring the dark places helps us work out our fears, whether active or latent, and then empowers our curiosity to discover another aspect of God's illuminating love.

What Kind of God Would Do This to Me?

Sooner or later, most people who suffer get philosophical. They ask questions about why bad things happen to good people like them. They ask how God can allow pain and suffering in the world. Some wonder if God is causing pain to teach them something or discipline them for something they have done.

These questions can become tricky. Does God allow pain and suffering to impact some people and not others? Or what about when an airplane crashes and some of the passengers survive? Did God save the survivors and turn his back on the victims who died?

I wish I could give you a simple answer, but I can't. That's because the answer is a mystery. No one knows for sure why differing measures of good and bad enter each one of our lives. And the topic of why some people endure repeated experiences of suffering is rarely addressed in sermons on Sunday mornings. I've attended a number of church services over the past three decades, and I can count on the fingers of one hand the number of sermons I've heard about this often avoided subject.

What I can do is review three of the most common approaches people take and assess their strengths and weaknesses.

1) God Is Love without Pain

Have you ever heard a TV preacher promise that God will heal *all* your pains and remove all your problems if you accept Jesus as your savior (and perhaps send a donation to the preacher)? Such promises are not uncommon when it comes to offers of salvation, but the problem with this approach is that it sells God as a big, heavenly grandmother who will shelter us from all harm.

Salvation is supposed to be accessible to all. The Apostle Paul tells us, "For everyone who calls on the name of the Lord will be saved" (Romans 10:13). We can signify our acceptance of salvation by simply raising our hands, or following our friends to church and signing a prayer card, or even pushing the right buttons on a computer keyboard.

I don't want to question what God can do or the means he might choose to transform the human heart from sin into holiness. But is raising your hand or touching a TV screen really all there is to it?

Perhaps we have diluted the message of salvation, neatly packaging the Christian life as a spiritual commodity for sale at a low price. German pastor and theologian Dietrich Bonhoeffer had a term for approaches that demand little of the believer but promise unlimited health, wealth and blessings. He called it "cheap grace," in part because we're in it to get the best deal for *us*, not to submit ourselves to the will of God.

The central symbol of Christianity is the cross, not a plastic smiley face, and the New Testament is full of passages instructing believers to turn the other cheek, or bless those who persecute you (Romans 12:14a).

Jesus never promised us a rose garden. We have to be careful not to take Christianity and twist it into a self-help cult that is all light and no darkness. The temptation is to intentionally skip over the cracks in faith that might lead us to the dark places in life. We would rather place putty over the mysterious areas of faith that do not exactly line up with our worldview.

The truth is this. God determines every part about our salvation. It is not simply based upon us asking Jesus into our hearts to save us from our sins, but rather, we have to be willing to give up our lives to Christ in order to connect with his Spirit and to share in a new life with him – one that is holy and purifying – one that is full of painful trials that grows our faith, promises us hope in the future and guides us on an eternal journey of love.

2) God Is Out to Get Me

The opposite approach portrays God as a cosmic bully who wants to throw us all into hell and in the meantime makes life as miserable as possible to teach us spiritual lessons. People who hold this view believe that the attacks on America on 9/11 were God's response to us for being too sinful, or too arrogant, or too gay, or too something. And smaller problems—like the coworker who bugs us—are interpreted as spiritual warfare, or karma or fate.

There have been times over the years that my own suffering has led me to wonder if God was disciplining me, perhaps because I had been too successful in life, complete with the salary and toys that signal success. Perhaps I had become too prideful and boastful, and he wanted to bring me down a notch or two.

Yes, there are times when all of us may feel that God is picking on us, but that doesn't mean we should adopt a "cosmic bully" image of God that fails to capture the true picture of God's mercy and grace.

3) Life Isn't Perfect

I have sought any reasonable explanation for my two decades worth of physical suffering. My search has taken me through various theological schools and dozens of pat answers. In the long run, I have been forced to conclude that we live in a fallen, broken world that results in each one of us experiencing pain and sorrow.

Pain may feel like a form of divine punishment, but God's discipline is meant for our good, not our loss. His guidance is designed to keep us on track during our walk of transformation.

It is difficult to explain this mystery, but let me illustrate by looking at water. We all need it, but not all water is equally good, and sometimes in our foolishness we prefer to drink the contaminated stuff. God knows we need the pure, clean water, and his discipline acts like a filter to separate the toxins from the nutrients so that instead of relying on a polluted stream to gather our drinking water, we are moved to look for the pure source. His ways bring us living streams of water into our souls so we can prosper during times of famine (Jeremiah 17:8).

No one can say why I might have more physical pain in my life than the next person. No one knows why you face the specific challenges you face. But we do know that God is with us in the midst of our pain and challenges. He meets us in the place of darkness, the place of suffering. It is in this place that salvation resides.

Darkness is a place where our inner person becomes renewed day by day and our purpose grows clearer and where we discover what the will of God is for our purified lives. If we can take our eyes off the form of suffering we're enduring and focus instead on the bright possibilities offered to us through the riches of our faith, then we will not become lost in the darkness.

Further, during our repeated visits to dark places, spiritual changes become more apparent. The darkness does not seem as dark as it formerly was. The light of God shines brighter in our suffering because our eyes are opened to an expanded perception about eternal living, instead of being focused on the unmet expectations of a decaying world. The darkness is where we will find our cross to bear in life, and it is where we will find our salvation.

God loves us. God disciplines us. We don't know exactly how he does these things, but we know that he grows us, oftentimes through suffering, from a place where we first believed to a place of bona fide spiritual maturity. As we continue to be transformed day by day, some aspects of the "self" will fall by the wayside; but on that final day, we will see that God's love has won out, and that he disciplined us only as we needed and only for our good.

Praying in the Dark

The last time we visited Joseph, he was sitting in a royal prison, unfairly accused of seducing the wife of a high official. This was after his brothers had sold him into slavery. Not a great life.

But Joseph never gave up on God. He continued praying to God from the darkness of his prison cell. And God never turned his back on Joseph.

In time, the warden put Joseph in charge of supervising the other prisoners. As a result, he interpreted the dreams of Pharaoh's chief cupbearer and chief baker, who had also been thrown into prison for offending an Egyptian ruler.

Joseph had a powerful prayer life, and I believe this spiritual discipline gave him sharpened gifts of prophecy and discernment. He used these gifts to accurately predict that there would be seven years of abundance in Egypt, followed by seven years of famine. Before long, Pharaoh got wind of these interpretations and asked Joseph what he should do if a famine were to strike the land. Joseph advised Pharaoh to save for a rainy day. Specifically, he advised the ruler to store surplus grain during the years of plenty, in preparation for the years of famine. That's exactly what Pharaoh did.

As a result of Pharaoh trusting Joseph's advice, Egypt was saved and Joseph was released from prison. The Hebrew derivation of Joseph's name is, "God increases or adds to." That's exactly what happened. He was once treated like a prodigal, but now he was favored. He lived in darkness of despair, but then he was brought into the light of day. Pharaoh handed him a signet ring, which symbolized Joseph's promotion to the number-two position in the Egyptian kingdom.

Joseph oversaw the kingdom's operations to store surplus grain. His oversight not only rescued the nation of Egypt from danger but also helped the house of Israel accumulate great wealth and prosperity.

Up from the Darkness

Joseph's story is so powerful because his ups and downs mirror our own journey of rebirth and transformation. We enjoy seasons of prosperity, joy and visible growth. But, during other seasons, we experience utter darkness. At these times our pain and feelings preoccupy us and hinder our ability to pray to God and thank him for his many blessings.

No one would choose to dwell only in the dark places of life, but any moment we spend in darkness is an opportune time to deepen our prayer life. Sure, you can pray for deliverance and healing. You can pray for the pain to end. At times, God will richly answer these requests.

But at other times, all we have is the darkness of our situation and the seeming silence of God. At those times, we should ask God not for a *way out* of our problems but a *way in* to the deeper realities of the spiritual life. If we do that, God will be with us and help us grow in our love.

When some people find themselves in darkness and silence, they want to liven things up with distracting TV shows or movies. May I suggest that it is better to remain quiet, not making yourself deaf to God's whispers. Prayers in the dark are powerful! They take us beyond mere words. They prepare us for higher purposes and for the challenges that lay ahead in our journey of transformation.

Beyond the noise of our pain is a vast kingdom of solitude, where silence, darkness and the unknown mysteriously coexist. There are times when it feels we have been forced into the darkness against our will, and we will do anything to avoid it. But now when I find myself in the darkness once again, these dark places provide me with a soundproof room to intently listen to what God wants to communicate to me.

The way things are, you will probably find yourself in darkness again before long. What will you do when you wind up there? Are you willing to take some time to listen? Do you hear him?

In the stillness, the Spirit of God turns up the volume button in our hearts. Listen for him. The next step is yours!

"Ask, and it will be given to you; seek, and you will find; knock, and it will be opened to you" (Matthew 7:7).

Insights for the Journey

- Your journey of transformation is never finished. Inevitably, you're going to experience additional challenges in life that will take you back to the dark places of your soul.

- Get back up and dust yourself off. Look at the dark times differently. Instead of automatically assuming that these sullen seasons are meant to punish you, consider the dark times as an opportunity to develop a clearer understanding of your faith.

- Darkness helps you to take your eyes off yourself and the world around you. It is a place where you can grow in your attitude of dependence upon God.

- God disciplines all those whom he loves and who belong to his family. Entering into salvation is the first step of spiritual transformation. Keep going, though you might have thought you've already arrived. Be willing to navigate through the darkness to find your ultimate purpose and to experience the fairness of God's love in an unfair world.

- In the dark places, the power of your prayer life can be realized. Learn to listen instead of rambling on with a plethora of requests. Take the opportunity to have your prayers purified for higher purposes.

Acknowledgements

I am grateful for the chance to write this book and for the help I received from so many along the way.

My beautiful wife Cherise has been my confidante and my best friend throughout our life together, and she has spent countless hours reading, critiquing and improving this book.

Cherise's mother, Bettye, deserves her due credit, as she has been the consummate cheerleader on my team.

Being a father to my sons, Jake and Kris, has been one of the true highlights of my life. During the difficult times of writing this book, I drew inspiration from the love we have shared over the years.

My dad has sacrificially shared his pair of eyes to give constructive encouragement. Both my parents are being acknowledged for their love and support of me.

Troy Uehling and Ron Banta generously offered their scrupulous attention to detail to provide the final proofread edits.

Father Michael O'Donnell has been a loving friend and guide who helped me get started on this project and connected me to people who would help me along the way.

Steve Rabey, a prolific author, most faithfully labored alongside me to transform my passion into the book you now hold in your hands.

God not only instigated my "Journey of Transformation," but also guided the entire process of turning my experiences into lessons that I pray may help you on your own journey.

About the Author

Dr. Gordon Selley, DC practiced chiropractic healthcare in the state of Colorado for nine years. After sustaining permanent neck injuries in 1994, his life-journey has taken him on an extraordinary path of transformation, ranging from total disability to getting back into the work force as the Chief Operations Officer of Selley Group Real Estate, LLC.

Gordon's comeback pursuits for a bona fide vocation have not fit the stereotypical career track of a "healthy" individual. His many physical limitations have prevented him from returning to the deepest passions he holds: working as a doctor to help those who are ailing among us.

As a result, Gordon has courageously walked the narrow road, in which he has literally gone from a bed-bound existence to totally reconstructing his life. From his 18-year journey (so far), Gordon has found another way to express his desires of helping others who are living with chronic pain, who are overweight, or who have succumbed to mental defeat and have lost hope.

Gordon Selley is a trailblazer for spiritual transformation. He is an author, mentor and speaker.

Gordon currently lives in Colorado Springs with his beautiful wife, Cherise. His oldest son, Jake, and his wife, Rebecca, live in Sydney, Australia. Kris, his younger son, is matriculating through his undergraduate studies at the University of Colorado at Colorado Springs.

Keep up with Gordon's blogs and video posts, or join him on facebook and twitter, or *schedule him for a speaking engagement*, by visiting:

www.gordonselley.com

Welcome to the "Journey of Transformation!"

Welcome to the Journey of Transformation

Personal Facts

Before	After
Weight: 225 lbs	Weight: 160-163 lbs
Waist: 42"	Waist: 32"
Neck: 18.5"	Neck: 15"
Shirt Size: XL-XXL	Shirt Size: S to M

Blood Chemistry Lipid Profile

	Before	After	Normal Ranges
Triglycerides:	*292	88	<150
Cholesterol:	*281	146	<200
HDL Cholesterol:	48	40	41-58
LDL Cholesterol:	*175	88	<129